DATE			

BAKER & TAYLOR

DEADHOUSE

JOHN TEMPLE

University Press of Mississippi / Jackson

DEADHOUSE

LIFE IN A CORONER'S OFFICE

www.upress.state.ms.us

The University Press of Mississippi is a member of the
Association of American University Presses.

13 12 11 10 09 08 07 06 05   4 3 2 1

∞

Library of Congress Cataloging-in-Publication Data

Temple, John, 1969–
  Deadhouse : life in a coroner's office / John Temple.
    p. cm.
  Includes bibliographical references.
  ISBN 1-57806-743-X (cloth : alk. paper) — ISBN 1-57806-744-8
(pbk. : alk. paper)
  1. Coroners—Vocational guidance. 2. Medical jurisprudence—
Vocational guidance. I. Title.
  RA1027.T45   2005
  614′.1′0922—dc22   2004020423

British Library Cataloging-in-Publication Data available

CONTENTS

PREFACE

I began spending time at the coroner's office in the fall of 1999. Most of the events of this book occurred in the summer of 2000. Dr. Cyril Wecht and Chief Deputy Coroner Joe Dominick granted me complete access to the coroner's office and its functions. They asked me only to respect the wishes of employees who did not want to be part of the book; one employee asked to be left out.

As a result of the generous access, I directly observed almost all of the scenic detail and dialogue in the book. I used a tape recorder and notebook extensively. I was not present for a handful of scenes, which I pieced together afterward through interviews, documents, and newspaper reports. Thus, when characters in the book say something, I either observed it directly or, in a few cases, they told me soon afterward what they had said. When a person in the book is said to be thinking something, that is based on interviews with that person. The book contains no composite figures or altered timelines. No names have been changed.

Without the support of the following people, I would never have begun or completed this book. Special thanks to my friend and mentor Patsy Sims, who made this path seem possible; to my mother and writing buddy, Loranne Temple, who inspired me by example; to my wife, Hollee Schwartz Temple, who never questioned the sacrifices required to finish this book and who, despite her squeamishness, read and improved every page; and especially to my father, Daniel Benson Temple, for his enthusiasm and faith.

I also owe thanks to the many other people who encouraged, counseled, and read drafts along the way, including Bruce Dobler, Diana Finch, Craig Gill, Michael Helfand, Max Houck, Dr. Jennifer Jackson, Deane Kern, Ellen Placey Wadey, Priscilla Rodd, and Lillian Thomas.

Thanks also to all the employees of the Allegheny County Coroner's Office, especially Cyril Wecht and Joe Dominick. It takes a special kind of confidence to give a journalist this kind of freedom—a confidence that comes from doing a job well. And special thanks must go to the main subjects of the book: Mike Chichwak, Ed Strimlan, Tiffani Hunt, Tracy McAninch, and Dr. Bennet Omalu. They were extremely generous with their time and patient with my endless questions. They do sensitive and important work, and they do it well. It was a privilege to observe them.

DEADHOUSE

ONE

TRACY'S FIRST NIGHT

Fifteen minutes ago, Tracy McAninch saw her first dead body. Now here she is, a summer intern, riding with a death investigator to confront a second one. In the backseat of the aging red Chevy Blazer, Tracy tries to prepare for what's coming: an old lady, dark patches on her neck . . . possibly murdered. That's all Tracy knows. She wonders if there will be blood. She wonders how she will handle it.

Up in the driver's seat, Mike Chichwak is whistling along with the jazz on the stereo, squinting at the scrap of yellow paper he wrote the directions on. The Blazer crosses a river and weaves through flat streets crowded with row houses, churches and taverns, past an asphalt basketball court.

Tracy knows, of course, that she'll see plenty of bodies during her internship at the coroner's office—she just hadn't expected quite so many, quite so soon. Her first shift at the coroner's office began half an hour earlier. She was still meeting folks when a deputy coroner asked her to help him turn a body over to a funeral home director. The deputy wheeled a gurney into an elevator, and Tracy rode down with him, feeling jumpy right next to that bright blue plastic body bag.

And then, unexpectedly, in the garage, the funeral director unzipped the bag to check the identification bracelet. Tracy saw her—the sleeping face and the limp arm. The deep incision that began below her shoulder and headed for the stomach—the autopsy cut. Tracy knew the woman had felt no pain,

3

but nevertheless she winced. How could such a brutal cut not hurt? The case file said the dead woman was thirty-eight years old and a heroin addict. Tracy hadn't expected such a young corpse. She stared at the body, and a childish horror-image popped into her head: the dead woman sitting up on the gurney, just blinking and awakening.

Moments later, Tracy is swept into this new call, the old lady found dead in her home. Police found the marks on her neck and thought the woman might have been strangled. The young black deputy coroner, Tiffani Hunt, reminded the older white one, Mike Chichwak, to take along an elderly-abuse check-sheet, saying quizzically, "Why's someone want to hurt Grandma?"

A whole gang of people—deputy coroners, a doctor, Tracy, another summer intern—headed down to the basement garage. They took two vehicles—Mike drove his Blazer, and Tiffani took a white van they called the wagon.

Now, the street tilts upward and the Blazer begins climbing a steep hill, the coroner's wagon trailing. As they wind up the hill, the city rises behind them and the streets grow narrower. Greener, too, though very different from Tracy's semi-rural neighborhood northeast of Pittsburgh.

Tracy wonders if the sight she's about to see will change her.

Tracy McAninch is tall and gangly, all adolescent elbows. Her face scrunches up in alarm when she sees something gross, and she says "wow" a lot. Someone has given her a deputy's uniform shirt several sizes too big, and the white shirt billows around her narrow frame. After meeting her, one deputy coroner muttered to another that the interns seemed to be getting younger and younger. "What is she, fourteen?"

Tracy is twenty, one of a dozen college students starting summer internships at the coroner's office this week. Another intern, Carey Welch, sits beside her in the Blazer's backseat. Tracy wants to work in a crime lab someday and figures this is a step in that direction. Not the antiseptic side of science, which she likes—the test tubes and the slides—but a hard step, one that involves actual blood and gore and stink.

The dead woman Tracy is going to see lived in the neighborhood known as the South Side slopes. The South Side lies alongside the Monongahela River, and most of its residents live in the flats. Up the hill, the streets narrow and the frame houses are tall and thin, several hundred of them clinging to the slopes, clustered here and there, wherever the Germans who settled the hills could flatten out a broad enough terrace to pour a foundation. It is a city neighborhood, spotted with fireplugs and graffiti, but patches of woods survive on the steepest parts and rabbits hop along the streets.

Mike passes streets with names like Pius and Opporto and Magdalene. Crowning the hill is St. Paul of the Cross Monastery, a 150-year-old Romanesque-Gothic church surrounded by monastic buildings and a large garden. From their mountaintop garden bordered with honeysuckle, the monks of St. Paul can contemplate the breadth of Pittsburgh, the jutting skyscrapers wedged between the Monongahela and Allegheny rivers, the blanket of buildings and parks and roads that spreads in each direction over the hills.

From the Blazer's backseat, Tracy spots a police car sitting on a narrow street that borders the weathered brick wall of the monastery garden. Five middle-aged women huddle on the green stoop of a nearby house. The pavement is wet and the air is fresh on this early June afternoon, washed clean by a recent shower.

Mike parks near the patrol car, followed by Tiffani in the wagon with its black lettering: ALLEGHENY COUNTY CORONER'S OFFICE. The coroner's wagon attracts a lot of funny looks from people on the street. Curious glances, but guarded, wary: *Don't come for me.* The deputy coroners are used to it.

Dr. Bennet Omalu, the pathologist, climbs out of the wagon and approaches the interns. He is thirty-one years old and nearing the end of a one-year fellowship at the coroner's office. Shorter than Tracy, his large, round head suits his large, round eyes—innocent looks belied by his playful grin.

"You guys are having fun on your first day, huh?" he says to the interns, his Nigerian accent singsongy yet staccato. Tracy groans a nervous assent.

The city police homicide commander had requested that Bennet ride along with the deputy coroners. That way, Bennet can inspect the body at the scene, instead of waiting for the autopsy, which is the usual procedure. If Bennet thinks it's a homicide, the detectives can get a jump start. The coroner's officials are used to working alongside police, although their jobs involve different goals. Homicide detectives find the person who ended the life. Coroners figure out *how* the life ended.

Having a pathologist on the scene can prove handy. A month ago, the homicide commander had asked Bennet to come to the home of a forty-one-year-old woman found dead in her living room. The detectives were suspicious because of the woman's age and the fine black furrows etched into the skin of her face. The marks looked almost deliberate, like crude hieroglyphics. Bennet took a good look at the marks and declared them the work of cockroaches. If a human being had caused the marks, Bennet explained, they would have been surrounded by abrasions, and they probably wouldn't have been clustered around the eyes and ears. Cockroaches, with their powerful mandibles, can leave marks that look like abrasions or chemical burns.

Bennet was right. The next day, when they popped the woman's skull in the morgue's autopsy room, Bennet found a black patch of clotted blood. Stroke, not murder.

At the old lady's house, Mike tells Tracy and Carey to wait on the sidewalk while they go inside. No sense in novices traipsing into a house that could turn into a crime scene.

Bennet and the two deputy coroners nod to the women on the front porch, stepping past them and into the living room. The police and the body are in the bedroom at the back of the house, but Bennet begins taking mental notes as soon as he enters. Good death investigators often view the body last, first taking in the surroundings. The house is tidy, except for an area near the doorway where a small wire bookshelf lies on its side, knickknacks scattered around it. Something caused this disarray, the cops have surmised, because the rest of the house is so orderly and clean. Moving down the hall toward the body, Bennet passes a bathroom. The commode was not flushed after its last use. He takes care to sidestep a pair of knotted panties lying on the hallway's fuzzy pink carpet. All these things are clues, but their interpretation depends on what the corpse reveals. The evidence could point to rape-homicide; it could mean something else entirely.

The dead woman lies on her back. She's narrow-shouldered, skinny, and naked. Froth comes from her mouth, and bluish patches discolor her neck. She was eighty-two, the cops say. They're worried about the dark blotches on her neck. They look like bruises.

Bennet straddles the body for a closer look. He can tell immediately that the marks on the neck are not bruises or strangulation marks but decomposition, something he's seen hundreds of times. There are more patches on her stomach, below her ribs and above her angular hip bones. The question is, does the decomposition obscure the marks of a killer?

Bennet massages the old woman's neck, cool as porcelain through his latex gloves. He probes the cartilage that covers the thyroid gland for splits that could indicate strangulation. Nothing. The thyroid is tight and mobile. The neck shows neither the thin dark line that a garrote would have made on her neck nor the larger bruises or fingernail gashes from choking hands. Her face and eyes bear no pinpoints of red petechiae—the hemorrhages that occur in choking cases because blood is trapped in the head and pressure rises until the tiniest veins burst. Perhaps most importantly, her face, lips, and tongue don't have the swollen, reddish-blue look of a choking victim who has used up the oxygen in her blood.

Bennet flexes the dead woman's fingers and wrist to gauge the degree of rigor mortis. Judging from the decomposition, Bennet thinks the old woman has been dead for at least a day, probably closer to a day and a half. But not much longer than that, because her muscles aren't entirely slack, and the last traces of rigor usually vanish after thirty-six hours or so.

Tiffani has talked to the women on the doorstep, the dead woman's niece among them, and they said she suffered from a seizure disorder. A bottle of seizure medication was found in the medicine cabinet. No suicide note in the house. Elderly suicide victims usually leave a note.

Bennet is piecing together a series of events with these clues, and the scenario does not include strangulation. Not that murder is out of the question; Bennet knows that homicide plagues the young and the old more than the middle-aged. But he doesn't think that's the case here.

"Hey, doc?" Mike calls.

"What?" Bennet says.

"Here's a pill here on the bed," Mike says, holding the white tablet between his gloved fingers. Another clue. The picture is fairly complete. This is what Bennet sees:

The old woman felt the early symptoms of an oncoming seizure. Muscles throughout her body clenched, which gave her a constricted feeling, an internal pressure that made her need to go to the bathroom. She took off her panties in the hallway. The old woman kept a neat house, so the pressure on her bowels had to be intense for her to just fling them aside like that—she probably expected to pick up the panties immediately afterward. But the seizure symptoms increased while the old woman was using the toilet, and she went for her medicine. She had no time to put her clothes back on. Her lungs heaved, mixing fluid and air into the froth that bubbled from her mouth. She stumbled around the small house in the early throes of seizure, knocking over the wire bookshelf and losing the pill in her bedsheets. Then she died.

Of course, Bennet could be wrong, and likely *is* wrong about some details. But he believes the autopsy will support his deduction of no rape and no homicide. Meanwhile, police will wait. They won't turn this into a homicide investigation without good reason. If someone killed the woman, the body will bear evidence, and there's none as of yet. So the shoe-leather investigators will turn this one over to the scientists for now.

In the autopsy room, the body will be stripped, opened, turned inside out, emptied. Blood, urine, ocular fluid, and bile will be sucked out, dehydrated, atomized, and scanned. Organs will be cut loose, diced, shaved into sections less than a cell thick, saturated with dyes, eyed through microscopes. If it's murder, the evidence will show when the autopsy techs cut her open. Or when the labs find toxins in the blood or urine, or when the kaleidoscope-like organ tissue slides give up the ghost. With little delicacy and much painstaking science, pathologists will hone or reverse the findings made by investigators at the death scene. This process will start tomorrow.

While Bennet and the deputies investigate, Tracy and Carey stand on the sidewalk outside the old lady's house, trading histories. Both are from the Pittsburgh area—Carey the city, Tracy the suburbs—and both go to small private colleges in Pennsylvania. They will be paired throughout the summer, working two shifts a week, Monday evenings and Tuesday mornings. This schedule lets interns follow cases from death scene all the way through the autopsy the next morning. A dozen or so additional interns will work other days of the week. The administrator who interviews the interns usually tells them to think it over for a day or two before committing to a summer at the morgue. Tracy followed this advice, calling him back later to say yes.

Carey, however, told the administrator right then that she didn't need a day; she knew she wanted to do it. Carey is twenty-one, short, and curvy next to rangy Tracy. Her blue eyes and auburn ponytail also contrast with Tracy's dark eyes and hair. Carey thinks she wants to work in pathology or a DNA-related field, perhaps even go to medical school, and she's viewing the summer as a tryout, a chance to see if she likes this line of work. She loves watching surgical documentaries on television, doctors and nurses with bloody gloves, working wrist-deep inside a patient's body. But she's worried about whether she can handle the bad smells on the job. Most interns are like Carey, eager to get started. Many are forensic pathology buffs—they've read the books and watched the TV shows. Tracy, who wants to do the different, but related, work of the crime laboratory, can't even watch a slasher flick without covering her eyes during the gory parts.

Tiffani exits the house and approaches the interns. She's a stocky young black woman with inscrutable features bunched in the center of her round face. She speaks in a low tone. "It's not as exciting as we thought. You guys can probably come in. It looks like a natural death. The bruise on her neck looks like decomposition, a little decomposed, not much. You guys haven't experienced a real stinker yet."

Tracy and Carey laugh nervously.

As they approach the house, Tiffani elaborates: "Someone saw the dark spots and said, 'Oh, she got beat on the neck.'"

Tracy is relieved by the news. She's not sure she wants to see a homicide just yet. Following Tiffani, she steps inside the small house, but she sees no body. A plainclothed man she doesn't recognize—probably a police officer—is sitting uninvited in an easy chair in the living room, and the pathologist with the thick accent is talking to him. Mike Chichwak is standing in a hallway, his broad back blocking her view. Everyone seems relaxed. Nothing smells bad.

Tracy follows Mike and Tiffani down the hall, and then she sees the body on the floor. Tracy doesn't stare at it, just gives it sidelong glances. An old lady, her eyes shut, head thrown back. Her lips sucked in like a toothless panhandler's. Body angular and naked, exposed.

Everyone is just standing around casually, like it's no big deal, which to them it probably isn't. Maybe it's the mellow environment, but Tracy realizes that she doesn't feel that odd. Mainly, she's relieved, glad that her first case is not the mother of a baby, or a homicide victim, or someone living in squalor. She's an old woman who has lived out her life and died of natural causes in her clean bedroom.

It seems like a person should be changed by seeing death. It shouldn't seem so natural, so ordinary. And it seems unimaginable to Tracy that she would feel OK with the body right there in front of her, but she does.

On the way back to the office, rain begins tapping the Blazer's windshield.

"Well, what did you think about your first body?" Mike asks the interns in the backseat.

"It wasn't as bad as I thought," Tracy offers.

Mike likes working with interns, explaining things. He tells them that a thin corpse, like the old lady, will sometimes mummify as it decomposes, losing moisture, drying out, turning black. This process takes place in dry atmospheres where bacteria cannot multiply or, as with this case, in selective parts of the body such as the fingertips and lips.

The rest of the old lady's body is decomposing through putrefaction— enzymes breaking down tissue cells and bacteria devouring the body from the inside out. Typically, signs of decomposition appear first on the stomach, where the skin turns red or green as bacteria begin to break down the large intestine. Dark spots often appear on the neck soon afterward, as happened with the old lady.

In most bodies, as internal decomposition spreads and gases build up, the outer layer of skin grows loose and slimy. Different organs decompose at different rates. The bacteria-ridden intestines begin to go within hours, but the prostate and uterus may be visible in a skeleton as much as a year later. Thus, even on a badly decomposed body an autopsy may yield results. Decomposition itself occurs at different rates—slower in water than in air, and slower in the ground than either. In high latitudes and elevations, well-preserved bodies have been found, deep-frozen since prehistoric times. In a tight, dry casket, decomposition may slow to a near halt as well. When pathologists exhumed the body of civil-rights leader Medgar Evers almost thirty years after his assassination, they found his body in near-perfect condition.

A fat corpse generally will bloat after dying, Mike tells the interns, because gases build up as the body fat begins to decompose. "So if you *have* to have a decomposed body, you want one that's starting to dry out and mummify, versus the bloating decomposition."

The girls laugh, leaning forward from the backseat to listen.

So far, Mike's deep voice has been matter-of-fact. Now he moves into grossout mode. "The bloating ones smell real nasty, and when you move them, the blisters have a tendency to break and you have fluid running all over the place."

"Nice," Carey says.

"Yeah, we're just now getting into the good decomposition season," Mike says. "A lot of older people don't have air conditioning, and it's stifling hot in their homes and after two or three days they're found, discovered from the odor."

The interns quiz him about this, and Mike launches into a story about an elderly man he picked up in the neighborhood of Lawrenceville. He'd been dead two weeks. Going up the stairs to the second-floor bedroom, Mike could hear an ominous buzzing. When he opened the door, the room was black with blowflies. Along the baseboard of the wall lay an inches-thick carpet of dead flies. They'd lived out their lifespans in the room, laying eggs and multiplying.

"We emptied three or four cans of flying bug killer into the room before we could get in," Mike says.

Tracy and Carey will hear plenty of stories like these. They'll hear how corpses crap, fart, ejaculate, groan, and twitch—pretty much everything but sit up and wink at you. As a matter of fact, every so often a corpse *does* wake up. In 1994, a hospital morgue worker in Albany, New York, was wheeling a laden gurney out of a cooler when he noticed the body bag was moving. He unzipped it to find that the eighty-six-year-old woman inside was still breathing, despite spending an hour and a half in the forty-degree cooler. He notified the hospital's emergency-room staff that the morgue had its first ever "code blue," and doctors revived the woman. As it turned out, the woman was found unconscious in her home, and the emergency medical technicians who responded had wrongly concluded that she had died. (Despite the occasional "awakening," deputy coroners tend to ignore the advice given in a U.S. Department of Justice handbook: "Check for pulse, respiration, and reflexes, as appropriate.")

The deputy coroners and pathologists and autopsy techs are glad to tell their stories. When a fresh group of interns starts work, everybody in the coroner's office is invigorated. The job seems fresh again, in all its drama and horror. Because you can see it on the faces of the interns, rookies who haven't seen a hundred shootings and drug overdoses and suicides. Old stories sound new. And the jokes—the jokes fly.

It's a kind of initiation, too. Novice homicide cops and paramedics undergo the same kind of unofficial desensitization training. The veterans show them bloody videotapes and tell them graphic stories and jokes and praise the ones who display the least reaction. Bodies are given shorthand nicknames: "the OD," or "the shooting," or "Grandma." Emotional distance is a good thing, a necessary trait, when you're dealing with death every day.

Back at the coroner's office, Mike shows the interns how to weigh and photograph the corpse. When he unzips the body bag to shoot the dead woman's mug shot, Tracy can smell decomposition, no better or worse than roadkill. Mike tells her the body smells stronger now from the jostling.

Mike zips the bag back up and swings open a heavy metal door, and an exhalation of chilly, smelly air fills the hallway. Tracy peers through the door to see a room the size of a big-rig trailer. It's the corpse cooler, Mike tells them. Stretchers cram the cooler like a jumble of bumper cars, some bearing body bags, some empty. Four clamoring air conditioners keep the temperature at forty-one degrees—cool enough to slow decomposition but not quite cold enough to freeze dead flesh. Mike maneuvers the stretcher into the cooler.

As Mike finishes, an administrator comes down the hallway, on his way home. "What's up, folks?" he greets Mike and the interns breezily. "What happened to Grandma?"

Mike explains, and the administrator turns to the interns: "See? If you have a seizure disorder and you're going to die, put some clothes on."

Everyone refers to the old lady as Grandma. Tracy wonders if her summer at the coroner's office will transform her sense of humor, whether she too will be full of jokes in the face of death.

As the day ticks away, the morgue empties out. The deputy coroners turn off the fluorescent lights in the investigative office and switch on the old brass-bottomed lamp that looks like it used to sit in someone's living room. The lamp casts a golden glow on the fake-wood paneling. The investigative office is the size of a small motel bedroom; four desks filled with computers, police scanners, and telephones take up most of the space. Hundreds of shoulder patches from police departments around Allegheny County—and a few from foreign countries—decorate the walls.

Three shifts of deputy coroners staff this room around the clock, and each hitch has its peculiarities. The night-shift deputies—working 11:00 p.m. to 7:00 a.m.—tend to be a little odd, perhaps due to all the late-night auto accidents, the dozes between calls. The day shift—7:00 a.m. to 3:00 p.m.—is when the coroner's office is most hectic, full of doctors and autopsy technicians and secretaries and supervisors. Officials and students drop in for autopsies and inquests. The daylight deputies hustle, but they're often escorting people around and making phone calls and doing the supervisors' bidding, not investigating cases.

The evening shift—3:00 to 11:00 p.m.—has a different character. Autopsies are done in the morning, so the autopsy techs leave and the pathologists hole up in their offices with case files. Everyone else trickles out around 5:00 p.m., and the deputy coroners have the building pretty much to themselves. Sometimes it stays quiet all night, and the deputies just play computer games, watch television, and bullshit. But as often as not, the good cases happen on this shift. The evening-turn deputies work more homicides than the others. Violence strikes most often when day is done.

The building that houses the Allegheny County Coroner's Office is easy to miss—a three-story stone chapel squatting amidst skyscrapers. Completed in 1902, the stone structure originally stood across Forbes Avenue from Henry Hobson Richardson's castle-like Allegheny County Courthouse and Jail, which is considered to be one of the most distinguished buildings of the nineteenth century. The morgue was built to resemble it, with its arched stone entrance, thirteen massive stained-glass windows, and notched cornices running along the roof. Inside, the building is lavish with ponderous materials—broad marble staircases, wrought-iron banisters topped with stout wooden railings, doors two inches thick.

In 1929, the county government was expanding and wanted to construct a taller, modern building on the site where the morgue stood. The morgue could be moved, it was decided. Engineers designed a causeway of interlocking beams that resembled tracks used to launch dry-docked vessels from shipyards into water. The six-thousand-ton building was jacked up twenty feet onto the causeway and Belgian draft horses harnessed to a winch dragged it, inch by inch, down a sloping city block. It took three months to move the building 297 feet, during which time temporary water and sewage lines to the building were kept running and the staff continued to take in bodies and conduct autopsies.

Now the coroner's office stands smack up against a nondescript parking garage, set back from Ross Street, where it's separated from the courthouse by a taller government building. In a way, the obscurity of the morgue's present location suits the office. To its employees, the coroner's office, with its $5.6 million budget, sometimes seems like the hidden branch of county government, an afterthought at budget time, repeatedly denied money for renovations to its deteriorating building. Maybe nobody wants to think about dead bodies or the office that takes care of them. And yet this small building, physically pushed aside to make room for an expanding government, is a crucial intersection between the city's political, criminal, and medical worlds.

The Allegheny County Coroner's Office wields more power than most coroners or medical examiners. In most jurisdictions, governmental forensic pathologists do autopsies, declare a cause and manner of death, and then hand off homicide cases to a prosecutor's office. In Allegheny County, when a homicide is declared and a suspect identified, the coroner's office issues subpoenas and arrest warrants and hauls defendants into the building for a preliminary hearing called a coroner's inquest, in the manner of the old English system.

Hundreds of lives and deaths glance off each other every day here. Cops, killers, lawyers, doctors—all cross paths in the coroner's office. Homicide detectives come to observe autopsies of deaths they're investigating. Or they climb the wide marble stairway to the third floor to testify stone-faced in coroner's inquests, where prosecutors and defense attorneys spar over evidence and police procedure. Reporters come for the newsworthy inquests and photographers snap pictures of manacled defendants on the "perp walk."

But the office is much more than a branch of law enforcement. When a public health hazard arises, the 111 employees of the coroner's office are often the first to identify it. Over the years, the coroner's office has urged homeowners to build fences around residential swimming pools and install carbon monoxide detectors, lobbied against beer sales to minors at a local stadium, coached police on how to conduct car chases more safely, and, most recently, helped identify a heartburn drug that may have killed a local baby.

When tragedy strikes, the coroner's office is often the main source of information for survivors. For instance, when a US Air passenger jet crashed near the Pittsburgh International Airport in 1994, workers from the coroner's office helped set up a temporary morgue and a sort of forensic assembly line in which they meticulously examined, described and X-rayed human remains from the crash site. Only one torso and two bodies were found whole; most were in fragments. But the workers found serial numbers on hip-replacement joints, made telltale matches in dental X-rays, and discovered sternum wires that indicated the bearer had undergone open-heart surgery. After twenty-nine days of matching remains with medical records, workers had physically identified 125 of the 132 dead, a number thought to be unattainable immediately after the devastating crash.

Dr. Cyril Wecht has run the office off and on for most of the past thirty-five years. Wecht is one of the most famous forensic pathologists in the world, a favorite of conspiracy theorists everywhere as the leading debunker of the Warren Commission report on the assassination of John F. Kennedy. When a high-profile death occurs, an attorney or reporter or fellow pathologist on the case is fairly likely to call the stone building in Pittsburgh to ask Wecht to lend his expertise. But these days, Wecht is directly involved in few of the day-to-day cases in the coroner's office. That work is done by forensic pathologists, autopsy techs, lab techs, photographers, and deputy coroners like Mike Chichwak and Tiffani Hunt.

Tonight, the deputy coroners and interns order wings and cheese fries from the Original Hot Dog Shop in Oakland, which Tiffani calls the "Dirty O." Tracy has never heard of it. There aren't enough chairs for everybody in the investigative office, so the interns sit on a table, their legs dangling, as Tiffani quizzes them about their backgrounds. Tracy asks Tiffani where she went to college.

Tiffani hesitates before saying, "I haven't graduated college." She keeps signing up for classes at Chatham College but dropping them, she says. She's been a sophomore for a year and a half, and she's worked at the coroner's office for a little more than a year, plus two summers. Her cousin works here and got her interested. Between work and her five-year-old son, she has little time. Tracy asks Tiffani where she lives.

"The Hill District," Tiffani says. Then she clarifies, probably thinking that this suburban girl wouldn't know that particular neighborhood—after all, she doesn't even know the Dirty O.

"The hood," Tiffani says. "The ghetto."

Like Tiffani, almost everybody who lives in the Hill District is black. Most of them don't trust the police—the *po*-lice—or anybody connected to the law. And to them, anybody with a badge is law, including deputy coroners.

Which sometimes puts Tiffani in a tough spot. Say she strikes up a conversation with a guy in a bar. As soon as he finds out what she does for a living, he's either scared off or it's twenty-questions time. He wants lowdown on the latest homicide. Or else he asks the trick question: Do you like your job? It's a trick question because there's no right answer. How do you say you like picking up dead bodies? Or taking a dead child from a mother?

The thing is, Tiffani *does* like the job. Parts of it, at least. The medical stuff. She also likes knowing the inside story firsthand. Like today, helping figure out that the old lady most likely wasn't murdered.

After a year on the job, Tiffani is used to death, but some cases are harder to forget than others. For instance, motor-vehicle accidents. Those and child deaths, which everyone hates. She has a five-year-old son, and with this job she's always behind the wheel. Which makes those cases different from drownings or heart attacks, things she doesn't worry much about at the age of twenty-one. But even after working at the coroner's office for more than a year, bodies ripped up by glass and metal and asphalt can still make her shudder.

Tiffani thinks those things affect *all* the deputies down deep inside. She just shows it more, that's all.

The investigative office phones ring at 5:45 p.m. Suspected overdose in the city neighborhood of Beltzhoover, a street called Lorna Way. Mike pulls down the rolled-up county map to find the street, and they're on their way. This time, the interns ride with Michael DeRosa, a small and lethargic deputy coroner with bright blue mischievous eyes and a boyish face. At the beginning of the shift, DeRosa, as the others call him, had queried the interns: "Have either of you handled dead bodies before?" No, they shrugged.

DeRosa also keeps asking the interns whether they've learned anything yet. He's friendly enough, but his tone is ironic, as if there's nothing to be learned here. Tracy doesn't know how to respond.

Lorna Way, it turns out, is nothing more than an alley with a handful of houses. When they get there the rain has stopped and birds are chirping. The interns follow Mike and DeRosa up a set of wooden stairs and directly into the apartment—no waiting outside this time.

A uniformed officer and a heavy-jowled homicide detective in plainclothes greet the deputy coroners and interns. The room is dimly lit and decorated in dark colors—gray carpet, black couch, a tiger-print cloth blocking the window. It *feels* like a drug den, clandestine and dim. The dead man is lying on his side near the couch, wearing black jeans, a blue T-shirt, and red Converse high-top sneakers. Tracy can't get a good look at him.

The detective runs down the case, and Mike takes notes. First off, the detective says, this isn't the dead guy's house. It belongs to a friend who is in the hospital. The dead man was just staying here. Two boys found his body an hour and a half ago; one of the boys is the son of the real owner. The detective figures it's a heroin overdose. In the kitchen garbage can, they found a crumpled and scorched can the man used to burn his drugs. The detective squats heavily and taps his ballpoint pen against the dead man's left rear jeans pocket. "The syringe is there."

The cops have searched the house but found no drugs or even an empty baggie. The drugs may be underneath the corpse, but, as protocol dictates, the police waited for the deputy coroners to come before moving the body. It wouldn't be the first time a dead addict's stash was stolen. The detective speculates that one of the boys may have been getting high with the dead man the night before and taken the drugs, either this morning or after the OD. But there's no way to prove it—just a hunch, based on the missing drugs.

Tracy and Carey follow DeRosa back out to the wagon. He pulls out a stretcher, hands Carey a small blue nylon kit and Tracy a fresh body bag. Folded into a crisp square, the long bag is bright blue and equipped with a zipper. It is made of tough polyvinyl chloride and is nearly impossible to tear, so that evidence won't be lost. Carrying it up the stairs is the first actual task Tracy has undertaken at the coroner's office besides holding doors. Back in the apartment, Carey stands with her hands on her lower back, elbows akimbo, watching. Tracy peers over Carey's shoulder, her lanky frame hunched, hands jammed in her pockets.

DeRosa pulls on a pair of blue latex gloves and begins emptying the man's pockets. First he gingerly removes the syringe. The other back pocket yields a wallet and a small address book, which Mike sits down on the couch to thumb through. DeRosa, his face gleaming with sweat in the stuffy room, rolls the man over with a small grunt.

Stiff with rigor, the dead man's left arm now reaches upward, like he wants one of the investigators to help him up. His goatee is graying and his hair is long and lank. Otherwise, it's hard to tell what he looks like because his features are squashed, his nose bloody and flattened from pressing against the floor. Red patches color his face. The patches are called lividity, and they're caused by the dead man's blood growing stagnant after his heart stopped pumping. Gravity had gradually drawn the red blood cells down to the lowest points of the body. Since he was lying face-down, that included his face. The tip of his nose and other parts of his face that were actually pressing against the carpet are white, where the vessels and capillary beds are squeezed. These red patches become fixed approximately eight hours after death, so lividity patterns may indicate whether a body has been moved after death. For instance, if the man had been found with the same red patches on his face, but in a face-up position, DeRosa and Mike might have advised the police to re-interrogate the teenagers who found the body. But the red marks match the dead man's position.

"He don't look so good," DeRosa says blandly.

The uniform cop chuckles.

Tracy bends over Mike to watch as he goes through his wallet. Mike finds a ten-dollar bill, torn in half. "I thought this was a real ten-dollar bill," he says, holding it up. "It should be five dollars. Disappointed? Yeah, I guess."

Tracy begins to giggle helplessly at the grotesqueness of it all, the dead man, the dim room, the desultory and nonsensical jokes.

Mike is digging change out of the man's pocket, clinking them down on the glass coffee table next to a cigarette lighter and a pack of Kools. He comes across an odd metal coin, larger than a half dollar. "What's this?" he asks.

The detective takes a look. "I think it was his Narcotics Anonymous chip."

No one says anything for a while.

Heroin abuse has swung up and down over the years, and for the last decade, it's been a drug on the rise—regular users tripled between 1993 and 1999, according to the Drug Enforcement Administration. Pure heroin is a white powder, but it's usually impurely processed, cut with additives that turn it dark brown or black and tarlike. It can be snorted or smoked, but most users inject. They sprinkle the powder onto a spoon or bottlecap or can, add water, and heat the mixture over a flame. Then they draw it into a syringe and find a vein. Addicts typically inject into the veins of the left forearm if they are right-handed, or vice versa, then switch sides when the veins become hardened and clogged, often due to the additives used to cut pure heroin. When the veins of the arm are unusable, they shoot into the feet, the thighs, or even the abdomen.

Within seven or eight seconds, injected heroin metabolizes into morphine and binds to receptors in the brain that suppress pain and produce euphoria. Along with the rush may come a warm flushing of the skin, dry mouth, a heavy feeling, a sick stomach, and itching. The user feels drowsy, brain-clouded. The heart slows. Breathing slows. And sometimes, especially when the user is drunk, breathing slows to a halt.

Coroners and pathologists look for needle marks, but they are not always apparent, even if the victim has just shot up. Often, but not always, foam is bubbling from the victim's mouth. In autopsy, lungs may be scarred and heavy with additives. Lymph nodes may be enlarged from struggling to detoxify drugs. Blood, bile, urine, and eye fluid are drawn from the victim, and toxicology tests may reveal a level of the drug that is considered lethal—or they may not; the body may have metabolized the drug to lower levels. Different people can tolerate different levels of toxins, so it can be difficult to tell with certainty that someone died from an overdose; as with so many cases, the pathologists and deputies resort to ruling out other causes of death. They can't absolutely confirm that the drug killed the user, but they will do their best to make sure it's not homicide.

"You want me to stick him here?" DeRosa asks Mike.

"Might as well," Mike says.

As Tracy watches, DeRosa unpacks the small kit Carey brought up from the wagon. On the coffee table, he lays out a probe that looks like a sewing needle, a red marker, and a digital thermometer with a thin, six-inch metal spike sensor. Then he pulls up the dead man's light-blue T-shirt, revealing a pudgy stomach, reddish with lividity.

Tracy can't hide her curiosity. "Do you mind me asking what you're doing right now?" she asks.

Mike answers: "He's going to do a liver temperature."

When Mike Chichwak is doing a liver stick with interns, he often demonstrates the process and lets them do it. This time, DeRosa does it himself. With a gloved hand, he feels for the hard ridge at the bottom of the sternum and then moves one inch down and one inch to the corpse's right. Then he pokes a hole in the skin with the needlelike probe and uses that hole as an entry point to shove the thermometer's spike into the liver. Fresh interns can't bear to violate the body this way, and will hold the thermometer at arm's length to distance themselves from the body. In this awkward stance they lack the force to puncture the skin, and Mike will tell them to stand closer. It's all part of getting comfortable with dead bodies, ridding yourself of superstitious fear. Death investigators must learn to view corpses as nothing more than evidence, like the scorched drug can or the syringe in the back pocket.

The man lies on his back, the thermometer jutting from his stomach like an arrow in a dead warrior. As they wait for the digital display on the thermometer to settle on a number, DeRosa draws a red circle on the skin around the thermometer's spike. The circle will let the pathologist doing the autopsy know that the puncture is from the liver stick, not foul play. (Later that night, doing another liver stick, DeRosa will offer the interns a helpful bit of instruction: "Never draw a smiley face around the liver stick hole," he says. "Somebody did that once and the bosses didn't like it.")

"Eighty-point-eight," DeRosa says now, reading the numbers off the thermometer's digital readout.

Normal body temperature, of course, is 98.6 degrees, which means the man likely lost 17.8 degrees since he died. In the first hours after death, as metabolic activity continues in tissues and bowels, temperature actually rises a degree or two, researchers say. The activity gradually ceases as the cells of the body die. This is a gradual process—brain cells die after only a few minutes of oxygen deprivation, but muscle cells may survive for hours or days. Eventually, however, the surrounding temperature takes hold and the body's heat begins to ebb at a rate of one-and-a-half or two degrees an hour.

Using the latter number and assuming the equation was exactly true means the overdose victim would have died about fifteen hours earlier. But it's not that simple. The temperature of the surroundings affects the cooling rate, so deputies must record that, too. A body lying on a cool concrete floor will drain body heat faster than on a carpet, which contains pockets of insulating air. Likewise, a naked corpse will cool faster than one wearing a winter coat. Also, the body temperature at the time of death is unpredictable. A person who dies from hypothermia will be colder; a person who dies from infection will be warmer.

To complicate matters further, the event that causes death and the actual death may be separated by hours. Say a person falls down the stairs and cracks his head against the floor, as a German businessman did a couple weeks ago. In that case in the southern suburbs of Pittsburgh, cerebral and spinal shock likely set in immediately, rendering him comatose. But the German may have continued to breathe and maintain body temperature for hours after the fall. Gradually, arteries leading to his brain dilated and his cerebrum filled with fluid. As the gray tissue expanded, veins leading away from the brain contracted, trapping more fluid in the skull and eventually suffocating the brain. Thus, even an exact time of death in that case would not necessarily give investigators the time of the actual tumble down the stairs.

Too many variables exist for an exact time of death to be much more than a guess. And that's why the coroner's office does not take body temperatures to gauge time of death. The liver sticks yield information for a research study one of the pathologists is doing, but it won't be used as evidence.

In fact, old-fashioned detective work at the scene pinpoints time of death more often than science. Deputy coroners or police check to see when the mail was collected last. Whether lights are on or off. The date the *TV Guide* is opened to. In figuring out exactly when the German businessman had died a couple of weeks ago, body temperature findings were inconsequential. Investigators decided he died sometime the night before. After a night of drinking, companions had dropped him off at the apartment he was using during a business stay in Pittsburgh. When he was found the next morning, he was wearing the same stylishly blended clothing he'd worn at the bar—black pants, gray shirt, and olive sports jacket. Clenched in his hand was a copy of the previous day's paper.

Done with the liver stick, DeRosa looks up at the interns, deadpan. "So what'd you guys learn so far?"

The girls laugh, and Tracy feels like she should ask a question. "How long has he been here?"

"He's starting to come out of rigor," DeRosa says. "Twelve hours?"

Mike and DeRosa unfold the body bag and spread it out on a more durable "reuse" bag. The reuse is made of heavy gray plastic reinforced with wooden slats. With highly decomposed bodies—bad stinkers—deputy coroners will lay down yet another sheet of plastic to wrap the body in. DeRosa and Mike position themselves over the body, bracing their legs wide. DeRosa grasps the legs, Mike the arms. They lift the body up a foot and swing it over and down onto the bag. The deputies fold the arms down by his side, zip up the body bag and strap it to the reuse bag. Then they cover the whole thing with a fuzzy maroon blanket embroidered with the words ALLEGHENY COUNTY CORONER'S OFFICE. The blanket helps deflect questions from curious bystanders.

The men grasp the reuse bag's handles, brace themselves, count off—*one, two, three*—and stand up. Mike has the upper body, DeRosa the legs.

"DeRosa always sticks you with the heavy end," Mike grunts to the interns.

"I got bad knees," DeRosa puffs.

Mike and DeRosa wrestle the laden body bag down the wooden steps and strap it onto a wheeled gurney on the sidewalk. As Mike shoves it into the wagon, the stretcher's legs fold up, scraping against the bumper, grooved from hundreds of similar loads. The deputy coroners strip off their blue latex gloves and toss them into the biohazard bin in the back of the wagon before shutting the doors. Then they squeeze globs of Lysol antibacterial gel on their hands and begin slathering.

Rain has begun falling again, and the sky is gray and dimming to an early twilight. The young men who found the body are smoking cigarettes underneath the balcony of the house.

Mike asks the smokers if they know anything about the dead man's family. One man wearing jeans and a sweatshirt says he thinks the dead man was from Texas. He says he's been calling bars, asking around about him. He seems to want Mike to know he's trying to help. Mike gives the group the coroner's office phone number, just in case. He needs to track down a next of kin, and any lead could help.

Thunder cracks, and everybody jumps.

From Lorna Way, Tracy and Carey ride with DeRosa to a suburban hospital to pick up another body, and Mike heads back to the coroner's office. Mike pulls into the garage beneath the stone turrets that tower over the rear of the morgue. He yanks the gurney out the back of the wagon and tows it into an antiquated freight elevator paneled with green-painted wooden slats. A scale built into the floor of the elevator is designed to weigh corpses and subtract the stretcher weight. When Mike rolls the stretcher onto it, digital numbers on the scale monitor zip up, down, up, then settle on 155 pounds. Mike jots the number down, shifts a gear handle, and the elevator lurches up to the first floor.

Upstairs, Mike rolls the stretcher past three stainless-steel postmortem tables and into a hallway. There he uses a video camera mounted to the ceiling to take a head-shot of the overdose victim. Then he shoves the gurney into the cooler for the night.

Soon, DeRosa and the interns return from the hospital with the body of a forty-two-year-old man who had collapsed at home and died in the emergency room. (At the hospital, DeRosa had pointed to the naked man. "I'm going to see how observant you are," he told the interns. "Is he circumcised or not?")

By the time DeRosa and the interns rejoin Mike in the investigative office, a *Friends* rerun is on the television and Mike is seated at his desk, thumbing through the overdose's belongings held in a plastic baggie: a tan leather wallet, keys, rings, and a driver's license. The interns sit on the table again, and DeRosa leans close to them and says in a low voice: "Watch Mike. He's a good deputy."

If Mike hears the comment, he shows no reaction. He sorts through a wad of business cards and phone numbers in the wallet, placing the bulk of them in one pile and separating four promising cards into another pile. The dead man's Social Security card. Two scraps of paper with handwritten phone numbers and names that match the dead man's last name. A business card bearing the name of the barbershop where the detective said the dead man worked. Mike wants to get someone who will know the dead man's family, not just a local drug buddy.

Mike dials the number of a woman whose last name matches the dead man's. No answer. He dials the number of a man with the same last name. After a moment, he straightens and says: "Can I speak to Ricky?" After a pause, he repeats the number he just called. "Do you know Rick at all?" Mike persists. Then: "Sorry." He hangs up, sighs and taps his pen on his desk.

Mike begins leafing through the palm-sized address book DeRosa found in the overdose's back pocket. He writes down the numbers of everybody with the dead man's last name.

He dials a third number. No answer. Mike doesn't put the receiver down, just clicks the button to hang up and dials a fourth number. Nothing.

A fifth. Nothing. He's run out of names that match the dead man's. Then he remembers that the slip of paper containing the number he called first also had an address—a Michigan address. Maybe the overdose is from Michigan.

Mike grabs a large telephone book and flips to the page that shows Michigan area codes. He jots down the area codes, tosses the book under his desk, then flips through the overdose's tiny phone book. He spots a number that begins with a Michigan area code and dials it. After a moment, he straightens.

"Can I speak to Sue or Brandon?" Mike says. He listens, then says: "Maybe you can help me out." He identifies himself and asks if the overdose's name sounds familiar. A moment passes, then he says: "I'm sorry, but he was found deceased this afternoon."

When Mike speaks next, his voice is gentler. "Our area code is 412 . . . OK, take your time." He gives the coroner's office phone number and repeats his name. He hangs up.

A woman answered, he tells the interns, and said she knew the dead man only as a friend of a friend. Nevertheless, she broke down crying right away. She said she would try to track down a family member and pass along Mike's phone number.

It's 8:00 p.m. *Friends* is over. Mike sits back in his chair to write the case story and wait for the call.

At fifty years old, Mike Chichwak is broad-shouldered, with a full head of wiry graying hair. When he's concentrating—searching a death scene, for instance—his eyes behind his tortoiseshell glasses often take on a slightly dazed stare. Mike was a Pittsburgh paramedic for thirteen years. Most of that time he loved the job, the rush of the sirens and lights, the adrenaline pumping on the way to the hospital, then calming down with a cup of coffee in the emergency-department lounge before heading out on the street again. But toward the end, when the adrenaline got to be too much, Mike decided to become a deputy coroner. When he runs into paramedics he used to work with, they ask him sometimes if he misses it. Mike tells them that his patients no longer vomit on him or curse at him.

Around the coroner's office Mike is respected for his persistence, the patient doggedness with which he pursues each case, big or small. It's a good quality for a deputy coroner, especially when you've amassed a ten-year body count the size of Pearl Harbor's, as Mike has. Because the smallest detail can turn a nothing case into a hot one.

Mike remembers the case of a man with a history of heart trouble. Police thought it was a natural. Nobody could locate a next of kin, so deputy coroners came to haul the body to the morgue. They noticed a tiny gold link lying on the carpet; on closer inspection they saw a suspicious mark on the man's neck.

This launched a full investigation, which revealed that the man's lover had strangled him, ripping off his necklace.

So cases aren't always what they appear to be. A recent *American Journal of Forensic Medicine and Pathology* article analyzed a decade's worth of death investigations in Fulton County, Georgia. The researchers found that death investigators and forensic pathologists disagreed on the manner of death in 12 percent of those cases. Twenty times, death investigators overlooked evidence such as strangulation marks, bullet wounds, and knife wounds and recorded those cases as natural or accidental deaths, only to have the pathologists conduct autopsies and discover that they were homicides. In one case, a driver inadvertently struck a pedestrian. The collision was tying up traffic and it was raining, so the investigator did a perfunctory examination before removing the body and classifying it as an accident. Pathologists later identified multiple gunshot wounds to the victim's head. By then, valuable time and evidence were lost.

Alternately, in twenty-one cases, death investigators reported homicides that proved to be accidents, suicides, or natural deaths. In one case, death investigators determined that a woman's body had been moved after she died, so they classified the case as a homicide. But the autopsy revealed she had died of a cocaine overdose. As it turned out, her friends had dumped the body to avoid the police.

A good death investigator has to catch the details. Like the old lady earlier today . . . the panties in the hallway . . . the clutter around the doorway . . . the pill on the bedspread. A good investigator always sustains an ember of skepticism that, fed with evidence, can turn into a blaze of suspicion.

The other deputy coroners also notice the way Mike deals with bereaved friends and families. This job deadens any genuine feeling of empathy, some deputy coroners say. At best, they're able to put on an act, lowering their voices in understanding when they call the next of kin. After hundreds of such calls, some veteran deputy coroners have a hard time even faking sympathy. But with Mike—who has worked at the office eleven years, longer than all but one other deputy—it doesn't come off as an act. Mike works at it. Over the years, he has become an expert at speaking to bereaved families and showing compassion. He speaks in a straightforward tone, without mincing words, but softens his normally strong voice. When he breaks the news in person, he often helps them sit down, and he crouches to be level with their eyes, trying to be nonthreatening. He will hunt down a bottle of carpet cleaner and scrub out a bloodstain so the family doesn't have to do it. Mike Chichwak is a strong-jawed, thick-wristed son of a railroader, with a vowel-flattening Pittsburgh growl for a voice, but somehow his compassion comes through.

Mike's father died three weeks ago. Seventy-six. Heart trouble. When Mike got the call from the hospital, he was working in the flower shop of the John N. Elachko Funeral Home, in South Oakland, a crowded city neighborhood. The funeral home has been in Mike's family, more or less, since he was a kid. First it belonged to Mike's uncle, who sold it to Mike's cousin. Then when Mike's cousin died, it went to his widow. A few years later, she and Mike began dating.

Mike grew up in nearby Greenfield, but he spent plenty of Saturdays hanging out in Oakland while his dad helped out around his brother-in-law's funeral home. His father's real job was at the Jones & Laughlin Steel mill on the South Side flats next to the Monongahela River. He was a car inspector in the mill's train yard. Thirty years he walked down the tracks, checking each car's coupling system and brakes, making sure everything was safe. Back then, Mike's father would drop everything on weekends to pitch in at the funeral home, or to help fix a buddy's car, or to lend a hand anywhere else for that matter. He was friendly and easygoing, and he liked keeping busy, traits Mike believes he has inherited. If the funeral home was busy, he'd help his brother-in-law in the clumsy struggle of dressing the deceased, pulling on the dark suit jacket and pants, knotting the tie just right. He'd help lug the casket to the viewing room and set out flowers. He'd guide the funeralgoers as they parked, a struggle in congested Oakland.

Inevitably, the funeral home was where Mike saw his first dead body. He was eight or nine, and he followed his cousin down to the embalming room in the basement. A dead man lay on the table, partially covered by a sheet. Mike was scared, but he also felt the tug of morbid curiosity.

Later, being around dead people came to be commonplace. Mike became an altar boy and served at funerals. As a teenager, he helped out around the funeral home when his father was busy. During his years as a paramedic, many of his patients died, sometimes before he got there. Now, as a deputy coroner, he sees death every day. And just like his father did, Mike now spends his off time helping his girlfriend run the funeral home, helping people park, dressing the deceased.

Mike's father had undergone a routine physical the previous October, and the doctor found clogged arteries. So a couple months ago, he had an angioplasty. A surgeon inflated tiny balloons in his arteries to open them back up. As his father recovered, Mike visited him most days, and was even late to work once or twice—late meaning getting there right around 3:00 p.m. instead of his usual half an hour early. His father seemed to be getting better day by day. One Sunday, he finished his entire lunch and took a walk around the hallways of the coronary rehabilitation center in the suburban hospital where he was recovering. It was the best day he'd had since the surgery. He was recovering.

When Mike picked up the phone in the funeral home flower shop three weeks ago, a nurse was on the other end. She told him that his father had taken a bad turn, and something clicked in Mike's head. Her voice carried a tone he recognized. A tone he'd used a thousand times himself. It wasn't just her words. She told him only that his father had passed out and that they were trying to resuscitate him.

Mike knew better than that. After all, he was a professional. He'd used that tone himself, at least a thousand times. As an altar boy, at the funeral home, as a paramedic, as a deputy coroner. Now it was coming back at him, one death professional recognizing the work of another.

He couldn't quite believe it yet, but as Mike climbed into his truck to head to the hospital, he knew what awaited him. More of those voices, breaking the bad news, using that tone, the one he'd used himself at least a thousand times.

That was three weeks ago. Now Mike is back at work, and strangely enough, tracking down family members to tell them that someone has died feels no different than it did before.

In the investigative office, the phone rings. The Michigan woman has come through. She passed Mike's number along to an old friend of the overdose, and he is calling now to give Mike the name of the dead man's brother, who happens to be a police officer in Plymouth, Michigan. Mike calls the Plymouth police and tracks down the brother's sergeant. The sergeant gets ahold of the brother, and, finally, Mike has a next of kin. But not just any next of kin. A police officer. So Mike wants to treat this case with extra care and respect. The brother seems in pretty good shape as Mike fills him in on the details. He says he will come to Pittsburgh in a day or two to make arrangements. Mike says he'll be here.

A few minutes later, a towering young man in blue hospital scrubs and bright white Etonic sneakers walks into the investigative office. He says he is from the Center for Organ Recovery and Education, known as CORE. He's here to remove the corneas of the man DeRosa and the interns picked up from the hospital an hour ago.

DeRosa lounges back in his chair as if he's too tired to get up. "I just put that guy in the cooler," he complains.

The organ center man waits patiently, a black duffel bag in one hand. Deputy coroners often complain about the organ center. They agree with the idea of harvesting organs for transplantation, of course, but they grumble that the organization is pushy and sometimes callous. They tell stories about agents hovering outside hospital rooms as families say goodbye to a loved one.

Finally, DeRosa gets the cornea donor out of the cooler. The dead man was forty-two years old. He was treated for lung disease a couple years ago, but seemed to be winning the battle—until 2:00 p.m. today, when a pain shot through his chest while he was at home with his wife. He collapsed and was pronounced dead in the hospital half an hour later. He is a tall white man with a big soft body. A tracheotomy tube juts from his throat where the emergency-room doctors left it, and gauze is taped over his eyes to hold his lids shut, so the corneas won't dry out. The pathologists prefer to get bodies with medical paraphernalia attached so they can determine whether the emergency room or paramedics acted properly.

Corneas, in addition to bones and skin, are removed for transplantation at the coroner's office. Internal organs are usually removed by surgeons at hospitals—by the time the body is at the coroner's office, it's too late. Organ-donation technicians usually extract bones in a sterile room in the basement, but the cornea extraction does not have to be a sterile procedure, so tonight the organ technician will do his work in the autopsy room.

Coroner's staffers have reservations about CORE in part because organ donation is a touchy subject. Morticians complain that the procedures disfigure bodies, which makes it difficult to do open-casket funerals. Cornea extraction can bruise the eye area, and leg bone extraction can damage the circulatory system, causing embalming fluid to leak from the vessels. The procedures sometimes take longer than expected, interfering with funeral schedules. In the mid-1990s, controversy arose when it was discovered that the coroner's office was donating brain tissue of suicide victims to researchers without the consent of the family. And just last month, a couple from an adjoining county sued CORE after they discovered that their son had been buried without his heart. The mother claimed that she gave CORE permission to harvest heart valves, but not the heart itself. Deputy coroners don't want to get caught up in a controversy like this.

DeRosa leaves, the interns stay to watch, and the organ tech grows chatty as he inspects the body, taking notes. The tech tells Tracy and Carey that he helps the doctors with large organ removals, but does corneas himself. The cornea is a clear dome of tissue that covers the iris and lens. It focuses light on the lens, which fine-tunes the ray of light onto the retina, a thin layer of nerve tissue on the back wall of the eye that converts the light into nerve signals that the brain interprets as sight. When the cornea is damaged and no longer transparent, a transplant is needed. The patient usually remains awake while the damaged cornea is removed and a new one stitched in place. The body rarely rejects corneas because of the limited blood supply to the area, so the operation is usually a success.

Once removed, the dead man's corneas will be stored in the eye bank for fourteen days, the tech says. They must be used before that. It's difficult to extract the corneas without damaging endothelial cells. The coroner's office makes this more difficult by asking organ center technicians to remove vitreous fluid from the eye before removing the cornea. Analyzing the fluid can tell pathologists what the deceased ingested in the last four hours before death and can help determine time of death, but removing the fluid damages endothelial cells. It's an example of the two organizations' different objectives: the organ-donation center serves the living; the coroner's office mostly serves history.

The organ tech asks the interns if they want to work in forensic pathology.

"This is what she wants to do," Tracy says, indicating Carey.

"I *think* it's what I want to do," Carey corrects.

"Have you ever seen a tissue donor?" the tech asks.

"No," Carey says.

"If you like autopsies, you'd probably like that," he says.

"I've never seen an autopsy either," Carey says. "We're still on our first day. We'll see that tomorrow."

The tech picks up the dead man's leg and begins flexing it back and forth— to get the blood moving so he can draw it, he says. The organ-donation center will test the blood for disease. Then he sticks a syringe in the man's upper thigh, searching for the thick femoral artery. If he can't get enough from the femoral, he'll try the subclavian, up near the collarbone.

Even as Carey ventures closer for a better look, Tracy remains at a distance. She stares at the syringe filling with blood, a crimson drop spotting the man's leg when the tech pulls the needle out. Her brain feels loose, dizzy. The needle looks so painful. How can it not hurt? But of course it doesn't.

"I'm going to step out right now," Tracy says, moving away from the body.

"You done?" the organ tech asks, grinning as he tosses the used syringe in a red biohazard box on the wall.

"Yeah, I'm done," Tracy says, reaching for the door to the investigative office.

Carey remains, tired but fascinated. Blood has never bothered her. Before today, she worried that smells or decomposition would. But this stuff she likes. She will watch surgical documentary shows for hours. Most of her high school friends in Pittsburgh can't understand why she chose to spend her summer at the coroner's office. But at least one of her friends, a fellow science major at Dickinson College, insisted that Carey call her with all the details.

The organ tech begins unpacking equipment from his black duffel bag. He pulls out a package containing two syringes, two scissors, two scalpels, two cornea storage jars full of a pinkish formula, and two plastic eye-caps, tan hemispheres that will fill out the closed eyelids after the removal. He removes the gauze from the dead man's eyes and smears a brown anti-infective solution around the eyes and nose and upper cheeks, giving the man a Lone Ranger mask. He unwraps a blue cloth with a hole in it and spreads it over the dead man's face so only the eye is exposed.

Donning size 8 latex gloves, the tech fits a small clamp over the left eye, forcing the eyelids open so that the gray eye stares unseeingly at the ceiling. He uses tweezers to pluck a bit of the tissue over the white of the eye so he can cut it with the scissors, which make a tiny *snip-snip* sound. Carey leans in closer to watch as he does this again and again until he has cut a circle around the cornea. As the minutes pass, the surface of the eye dries, losing its slick gleam. The tech makes some fine cuts with a scalpel, then snips with scissors. He is not pleased with the scissors—they're slightly dull and he may be damaging too many endothelial cells. But he works away and a moment later lifts out his prize—a morsel of transparent tissue that may soon be given another chance to function.

"There's your cornea," he says.

Dark falls over the city. The rain comes and goes. In the locker room next to the investigative office, water drips through a crack in the ceiling, gradually filling a garbage can set there to catch the leak. Around 9:30 p.m., the interns prepare to leave, tired from the long evening, the parade of corpses. Carey calls home for a ride, knowing her mother will be full of questions about her first day. Tracy is parked in a nearby garage.

Around 9:45 p.m., with a little more than an hour left in the evening shift, the phone rings. The night-shift supervisor takes the call and reports it to Mike and Tiffani.

Homicide.

There is some confusion as to the location—it may be Downtown. They wait for clarification. Tracy can't decide whether or not she wants to go to one more scene tonight. The deputies are waiting to find out where the body is. It's a homicide, so the deputy coroners can't wait and dump it on the next shift.

The phone rings again. They've figured out where the body is—a housing project called Addison Terrace. The Hill District. As Tiffani called it earlier tonight—*the hood, the ghetto.*

"Oh," Tiffani says. "The Hill. That's where I live."

It is decided that the interns will head on home. As Tiffani and Mike hustle off to the killing, Tracy says goodbye and heads for her car.

Tracy maneuvers through the dark, empty Downtown streets in her Toyota sedan, heading for the Sixteenth Street Bridge to cross and go up the Allegheny River, out of the city, and home. Images of the day flood her mind: the naked old lady with the bluish patches around her neck, the overdose guy in the red high-tops, blood from the needle spotting the cornea donor's inert leg. And now the homicide. She is curious to see a homicide, and part of her wishes she was heading up to the Hill District. But part of her is glad she is not. Of course, she'll see the homicide autopsy tomorrow. That thought makes her nervous.

Preoccupied, Tracy glances down for a moment, then looks up just in time to see that the light at the intersection before the bridge has turned red. Too late. Her car smashes into the side of a sedan.

Oh my God, Tracy thinks. *I just killed someone. I just killed someone, and now I'm going to have to take the body back to the coroner's office.*

But then, in the stillness after the crash, she can see two figures in the other car, and they are moving. They open the doors and get out and step away from their car. And relief flows over Tracy, relief that she won't have to see any more dead bodies tonight.

Meanwhile, Mike and Tiffani are driving to the shooting in the Hill District. The Hill is a long, irregular slope that overlooks the city's jammed triangle of skyscrapers. It was once a posh neighborhood, but it has been *the hood, the ghetto* for a long time. In the 1800s, it became the first stopping place for each wave of poor Pittsburgh immigrants—Germans, Scotch-Irish, Italians, Slovaks, Syrians, Armenians, Lebanese, Greeks, and Chinese among them. Those populations eventually moved east with the trolley line and the neighborhood was left to Jews and southern blacks, who began arriving in the late 1800s. For decades in the early 1900s, the Hill was a thriving Jewish neighborhood; head coroner Cyril Wecht grew up in a rented house on the Lower Hill near his parents' small grocery store, about half a mile from the coroner's office. But most Jewish families (including Wecht's) eventually moved a few miles east to Squirrel Hill, and by mid-century the Hill was all black. Jazz clubs thrived, and entertainers like Lena Horne, Billy Eckstine, Art Blakey, and Erroll Garner got their start here. It also became one of the most dangerous parts of the city, the geographic inspiration for the plays of August Wilson and the '80s television police drama *Hill Street Blues*.

Despite this vibrancy, Pittsburgh's black neighborhoods have been hit hard by the city's industrial decline. A 1994 study that compared Pittsburgh with fifty similar cities showed that the city had the highest poverty rate for blacks aged eighteen to sixty-four. The black middle class in Pittsburgh never developed the way it did in other cities. Partly, historians say, this was due to bad timing. The wave of black immigration to the industrial North, including Pittsburgh, crested between 1910 and 1930, just as the city's economic growth was beginning to slow down. Earlier white ethnic groups had taken advantage of the booming steel industry and established certain trades and jobs for themselves. Blacks came in great numbers at the wrong time and found themselves struggling to compete for the lowest-paying jobs. The city's topography played a role as well. Blacks settled in pockets in various parts of the city—the Hill, East Liberty, the North Side—instead of one major ghetto, which may have delayed their ability to organize politically.

And poverty led to crime. Last year, the Hill District endured four homicides, seven the year before that. Only one other city neighborhood— Homewood—suffered more, with nineteen homicides in the last two years. Deputy coroners don't always feel welcome at these death scenes, as many blacks in Pittsburgh feel bitter toward law enforcement. This resentment has worsened in recent years, partly as a result of the high-profile death of a black motorist named Jonny Gammage, who had been pulled over by a group of suburban police officers. A few years ago, twenty-five people, most of whom were black, sued the Pittsburgh police, claiming they were falsely arrested and illegally searched and attacked. The lawsuit claimed that police used "dragnet tactics and sweeping searches and seizures of young African-American males who reside in or happen to be present in communities where gang activities are suspected. . . . " In 1996, a newspaper survey revealed that almost 73 percent of blacks in Allegheny County believed that the justice system was biased against them, compared to 54 percent of blacks nationally.

A few weeks back, Tiffani was driving back from a case in the suburbs when she decided to drop by her house in the Hill to pick up some dinner. The dashboard of the wagon bristles with electronic equipment—CB radio, police scanner, cell phone, switches for the wagon's lights, and a siren, which the deputy coroners rarely use. When Tiffani is driving, the wagon is more likely to be pulsing with the heavy bass of rap music or maybe a little old-style Motown. Tiffani grew up in the Upper Hill, sometimes called Sugartop. She has family all over Sugartop, here a cousin's house, there an aunt's.

Just before she got to her street that day, she saw a cousin, Curtis Williams, tooling toward her in his rebuilt blue Nissan Pathfinder. Curtis also works as a deputy coroner. Tiffani pulled up beside her cousin's truck and rolled down her window.

"What's up?" Curtis drawled.

"I'm getting something to eat," Tiffani said.

"Y'all busy down there?" Curtis asked mischievously. He hadn't been at work since the week before, when he strained his back picking up a 300-pound corpse.

Tiffani shot her cousin an evil look and drove away.

Curtis is a good example of how tough it is to live in the Hill and be a deputy coroner. The year before, someone shot one of Curtis's best friends eight times. The man staggered to Curtis's door, rang the bell, and collapsed. Curtis and his mother, a homicide detective, gave CPR and called an ambulance. As his friend lay in an intensive-care bed during the next two days, Curtis took off work. He didn't want to be at the coroner's office when the call from the hospital came in. His friend survived, but three months later, when Curtis was getting off work one night, his mother called with bad news. Curtis' brother-in-law was dead, shot in the back of the head. Curtis went to the scene and helped remove the body.

After her brief chat with Curtis, Tiffani passed her son's elementary school, calling out to a woman she knows: *Hey, Mrs. B.* Then, to a group of kids: *What's up, y'all*. In her neighborhood, everyone lifts a hand to each other.

Ahead of her was her grandparents' home, an elegant three-story brick house with a high-peaked roof. The front yard was fenced in white and covered with ornamental lawn animals. A lot of the houses in this part of the Hill District were big and nice, but you could tell it was the hood because of the burned-out, boarded-up ones.

Tiffani's house was next-door to her grandparents', but smaller and simpler, paneled with yellow siding. Tiffani ran inside, grabbed her dinner, and took off again. Heading back toward Bigelow Boulevard, she braked to let a tall, gaunt man walk in front of the coroner's wagon. The man started waving his scarecrow arms in the air like he was afraid, maybe just kidding around.

"All right, all right," the man shouted. "This van is scaring me! Go on ahead."

"Don't be holding up the traffic," Tiffani called out as she blew past him.

Moments like that are why Tiffani doesn't like wearing the uniform home or taking the wagon to her neighborhood. The guy took one look at the wagon, and right away he thought *cop*. Or maybe he was thinking *death*. Either way, it's not always easy to work this job when you live on the Hill.

Three weeks later, Tiffani is heading up to the Hill in a coroner's wagon again, but this time she's heading to a shooting.

By the time Mike noses the wagon into the housing project's parking lot, the streets are thick with people. Black-and-gold-striped patrol cars are everywhere, their overhead lights rhythmically illuminating the dozen or so long, three-story brick buildings. Here and there, the windows on the building are covered with sheets of plywood. Between the buildings, sidewalks crisscross the courtyards, which contain open dumpsters, weedy basketball courts, and cyclone fences. And people: shirtless boys, old folks, women with babies on their hips.

Tiffani and Mike get out of the wagon and approach the knot of homicide detectives near the body. Uniformed cops patrol between the milling crowd and the crime scene, but they are outnumbered. And the mob is angry— grumbling and shouting. Tiffani knows that the crowd probably includes some of her friends or acquaintances or maybe even family. Nevertheless, she doesn't look over at the throng, and nobody shouts her name. They wouldn't bother her while she was wearing the uniform, working on the other side of the crime-scene barrier. Working with the *po*-lice.

The dead man sprawled at their feet is black. Tiffani would be surprised if he weren't. More than half of all homicide victims in the county are black males, and pretty much everyone in her neighborhood is black. Tiffani takes these facts for granted. One day, when some interns were looking up homicide cases on the computer, Tiffani told them: "If you're looking for a homicide case, look for a young black male." ("Tiffani's been looking for one for years," one deputy added, and Tiffani snorted.)

The method of killing is no surprise, either. Shooting is by far the most common way people kill each other—coroner's office records show that about 70 percent of the county's homicide victims in the last two years died by gunshot, as opposed to almost 10 percent by stabbing, 9 percent by beating, and 5 percent by strangulation. One person was killed by arson and two by intentional carbon monoxide poisoning.

The dead man lies face up, arms at his side, like a child feigning sleep. He looks younger than his twenty-seven years. He is handsome, with pale gray eyes and a trimmed chin beard. In the police flashlights, the bright orange of his shirt stands out against his black jacket and jeans. Two orange bandannas hang from his pocket—gang colors, probably. In the dim background, beyond the line of cops, the crowd mills and murmurs and curses.

The detectives tell Tiffani and Mike what they know, basically that there was an argument between the victim and a tall black male who pulled a small shiny pistol and fired one shot to the victim's upper chest. Forty feet from the body, the police found some blood and a .38-caliber bullet casing. The detectives figure the shooting took place there and the victim stumbled over here and fell.

But the crowd is getting ugly, the detectives say. They wonder if Mike and Tiffani would mind just making an extra-quick scoop and run—just get the body bagged and out of there as fast as they can, before trouble really starts. Mike and Tiffani agree. Forget the usual on-scene body inspection. This one is a clear-cut shooting anyway.

So it's over, extra quick. They bundle the dead man into a body bag, and haul him back to the morgue, where he'll spend the night in the cooler. At 9:00 a.m., autopsy techs will crack the cooler's big metal door and start fetching bodies for postmortem.

But that's tomorrow. For the evening-turn deputies—Mike and DeRosa and Tiffani—the shift's harvest of bodies is in.

TWO

AUTOPSY

This job has no doubt been around as long as civilization. Someone had to dispose of bodies, and someone had to scrutinize those bodies found dead in suspicious circumstances. Methods, however, have varied. In one Australian tribe, two men held a dead body on each end while a third tapped it with a green bough and called out tribe members' names. If the killer's name was spoken, the tribe believed, the corpse would convulse. Then came revenge.

In the thirteenth century, the Chinese wrote what was probably the first book of forensic pathology, *The Washing Away of Wrongs*. The guidebook was designed for local death investigators and contained some rules of thumb that still hold true, such as this advice about bodies pulled from water. "If in the nose and mouth there is watery froth as well as several small light-colored traces of bloody water . . . these are evidence of the deceased's having entered the water while alive." Although pathologists have for decades tried to develop a foolproof chemical or histological test for drowning, froth from the mouth is still the best indicator. Other advice from the book is less dependable. "When someone has been hanging from morning to night, even though the body is already cold, they may still be saved; if from night to morning, the operation will be more difficult."

The system of death investigation that eventually migrated to the United States began in late-twelfth-century England, when King Richard the

Lionhearted established the office of the crowner, a title that evolved into coroner. The job carried power because it initially was more concerned with money and land than causes of death. The coroner, usually a knight or landowner, investigated suspected homicides and suicides as a first step toward determining how the property of the deceased and accused would be divided. The king took a slice in these cases, and, always at war, Richard needed money. The new official would make sure he got his portion.

Over the centuries, as the crown found other ways to make money, the coroner devolved into a minor county official, paid thirteen shillings (and sometimes a meal thrown in) per body seen. When a body was found, townspeople stood watch over it until the coroner got there, often days later. (Sometimes this delay benefited the corpse, who would awaken. This happened often enough that the more expensive caskets of the day included a small flag that could be raised above ground from the inside, just in case the "deceased" woke up.) Once there, the coroner would inspect the body, summon a jury, and hold an inquest. This was a formal court proceeding, held sometimes in churches, sometimes in taverns. The jury gathered around the corpse and heard witnesses. Surgeons rarely took part, so judgments were made by studying the body's exterior. Superstition no doubt affected the outcomes—one common belief was that the corpse would spout blood if the killer came near.

The United States adopted the coroner system and, by the end of the 1800s, calls for reform and more emphasis on science heightened. In England, coroners were appointed and often were physicians or attorneys, but in the U.S. coroners were elected and usually had few professional qualifications. In rural areas, owning a wagon suitable for hauling bodies was a major requirement, along with a strong stomach.

As industrial cities grew, solving murders became more difficult. In small agricultural communities, the killer usually knew the victim. Husbands killed wives or neighbors killed neighbors, so a suspect was relatively easy to identify and find. In cities teeming with tenements, where strangers killed strangers, detectives needed all the help they could get, and they increasingly turned to science for answers.

But in many cities, coroner's offices weren't up to the job. Most coroner's physicians were from the lower ranks of the profession, and few were pathologists. Elite urban physicians led the call for reform of the coroner's office. Some demanded that physicians be elected to the office; others proposed abolishing the office altogether, punctuating their arguments with descriptions of botched murder investigations and autopsies. Medical journals regularly ran anti-coroner rants such as one 1902 article in the *Journal of the American Medical Association* entitled "The Useless Coroner."

Incompetence wasn't the system's only problem. At the turn of the last century, urban coroners in the United States possessed great power. They controlled the way evidence was presented to juries and ran detective forces that rivaled those of the police. Power led to corruption. Deputy coroners routinely looted bodies and collected bribes from undertakers. In some cities coroners distributed estates, sometimes embezzling a slice for themselves. If a wealthy woman died after an abortion or a politically connected man died in the wrong area of town, those details could be covered up for a price.

In response to the corruption and bad science, Massachusetts established the first medical examiner system in 1877. The difference was that medical examiners were appointed pathologists with special training in forensics and death investigation; coroners were often elected lay people who relied on medical personnel to do autopsies. Most medical examiner systems lacked the political power of coroner's offices—they were not elected offices and they did not serve subpoenas, hold coroner's inquests in homicide cases, or issue arrest warrants. After Massachusetts switched to an ME system, New York City followed suit in 1918, and after 1950 a flurry of medical examiner systems displaced or began overseeing coroner's offices.

Some places, like Pittsburgh, clung to the old coroner system by updating it and hiring qualified forensic pathologists to do autopsies. If all coroner's offices were like the one in Pittsburgh, which has had doctors running it for decades, fewer people would be pushing for a switch to ME systems. But in most counties, the elected coroner is not a physician. Many are undertakers, and some are in entirely unrelated fields. As recently as 1994, politicians have tried unsuccessfully to replace coroner's offices throughout the state with medical examiners. After being elected, county coroners in Pennsylvania who lack a forensic pathology background are required to take a forty-six-hour death investigation training course.

Well-trained forensic pathologists were scarce until a few medical schools began offering formal training in the 1930s. Physicians had testified in trials for decades, but most had seen only a few violent deaths in their careers and did not understand the science of stab angles, poisons, and gunpowder marks.

Throughout the last century, forensic medical training struggled to catch up with other specializations, perhaps because of its idiosyncrasies. First of all, its patients are dead, so instead of studying laboratory slides and live patients, budding forensic pathologists needed to work on bullet-riddled bodies. As a result, they worked in morgues, far from the hospital, a source of the medical profession's power. Even recently, forensic pathologists have complained that textbooks and training cover the medicine—injury patterns and pathologic changes—but not the practical stuff like how to check the lips of an overdose for medication dye or the proper way to mark and preserve a bullet fragment.

The Allegheny County Coroner's Office was no exception. In 1965, the *Pittsburgh Post-Gazette* ran a five-day series about the shortcomings of the coroner's office. The opinionated and lurid series, headlined "They're Getting Away with Murder," detailed suspicious deaths in which the elected coroner, a cabinetmaker with no medical training, had failed to conduct an autopsy. The morgue back then was primitive, equipped with little more than three ancient porcelain autopsy tables. It lacked even a microscope. One doctor later compared it to the laboratory in the movie *Frankenstein*.

Later that year, the county elected a new coroner, Dr. William R. Hunt, the first physician to run the office. Hunt hired Dr. Cyril Wecht as his chief forensic pathologist, launching one of the most storied careers in Pittsburgh history.

In the next three and a half decades, Wecht became the leading debunker of the Warren Commission report on the assassination of John F. Kennedy. He coined the phrase "the magic bullet," promoted the idea of a second shooter on the grassy knoll, and advised director Oliver Stone on the film *JFK*. He was arrested after a tussle with a city cop, hollered during county government meetings, was restrained from jumping into an election-night scuffle, and called one citizen who criticized him "an insignificant asshole." He waged bitter political campaigns for coroner, county commissioner, county executive, and U.S. Senate. In 1983, a judge ordered Wecht to repay the county $172,000 for using the coroner's office and staff for private autopsies and lab tests. (Wecht claimed the money was used to improve the coroner's office. In 1993, he settled the civil case against him, without apologies, for $200,000.) After that scandal, Wecht took a decade-long hiatus from politics before being reelected as coroner in 1995. During his time as a private forensic pathologist, he traveled the world to investigate or consult on death cases, from David Koresh to JonBenet Ramsey. He served as a running TV commentator during the O.J. Simpson saga and later lent his expertise to a Fox TV special called *Alien Autopsy: Fact or Fiction?* Along the way he conducted fourteen thousand autopsies, consulted on thirty thousand more, wrote numerous books, and gave up to six speeches a day, relentlessly promoting his passion for forensic pathology.

Less publicly, Wecht would revolutionize the coroner's office in Pittsburgh. In his first winter as chief pathologist, Wecht shivered in his overcoat as he dissected bodies in the building's unheated basement while new autopsy tables were being installed upstairs. Over the next five years, the coroner's office also bought thousands of dollars of new laboratory equipment—a spectrofluorometer, an X-ray unit, a gas chromatograph, and a camera-equipped microscope. Wecht eventually took over the office, hiring pathologists, toxicology and histology technicians, and photographers. He began training deputy coroners and autopsy technicians in the ways of death investigation. Before long, instead of performing just a handful of autopsies a year, the office was doing hundreds.

And they began diagnosing murders. In the decade before 1966, the coroner's office had detected a yearly average of thirty-nine homicides. Over the next five years, that number shot to sixty-one. The improvements couldn't have come at a better time. In recent decades, murderers and their victims are less likely to know each other, which means that police work is relying less on traditional techniques such as interrogation and more on science-based procedures such as examining trace evidence.

Today the autopsy room looks part surgical suite, part torture chamber. One long glass-front cabinet contains scalpels, syringes, scissors, knives, rib shears, bone wedges, mallets, forceps, rulers, plastic basins, cutting boards, latex gloves, test tubes, dissection jars, jugs of formalin. A bug zapper, a telephone, and a beat-up transistor radio sit on a table. A skeleton dangles in a corner, every bone labeled. Sometimes, a cigarette protrudes from its loose jaw.

The room runs the length of the rear of the coroner's office, above the garage where the wagons park, down a short hall from the office where the deputy coroners wait for calls. Fluorescent ceiling lights blast the long tiled room, drowning the meager daylight that filters through cloudy windows on the back wall. Three stainless steel tables stick out from that long wall. Faucets at the head of each table wash body fluids and scraps of tissue into a long single basin along the wall, where the pathologists dissect organs. A heavy-duty garbage disposal unit is attached to the drainpipe under the basin.

As Wecht has repeated countless times over the decades, if JFK's autopsy had taken place in a room such as this, with experts like the ones at this coroner's office, much more would have come to light and very different conclusions may have been drawn. The average shooting victim in Pittsburgh gets a painstaking and professional autopsy, a better postmortem than the president received in 1963.

The autopsy room is bedlam, bodies everywhere, alive and dead. Jokes and commands ricochet off the white-tile walls. Tracy McAninch jumps aside as a white-coated pathologist scurries past, carrying a glass jar with gnarled gray masses of tissue floating inside. A couple of pathologists shout across the room at each other, something about an "easy homicide" a few days earlier. An autopsy technician in blue surgical scrubs shoves a gurney through the room, and Tracy sidesteps again. There's nowhere to sit, nowhere that looks sanitary at least, and Tracy doesn't really have a job to do. She's also tired—she got little sleep after her accident last night, about eleven hours ago. So she just stands, hands jammed in her pockets, dark eyes darting around the room, and tries to stay out of the way.

Tracy is able to watch most of the autopsy of the overdose victim from Beltzhoover—the case she saw the day before—but she flinches when it comes time to cut. Especially the head. A tech slices the dead man's scalp so she can saw open the skull. After making the incision ear to ear in the back of the head, she pulls the scalp open, forcing the inverted flesh down over the face like a smooth red mask, hiding the dead man's features. Tracy sticks—her face transformed by a series of expressions from teeth-clenched horror to wide-eyed astonishment—until the tech picks up the handheld bone saw and starts to cut the skull. When the screaming saw blade bites into the bone, the saw makes a guttural grinding sound and kicks up a fine spray of ivory dust. The room fills with the dental-office smell of burning bone.

Tracy turns away with a sheepish-sick grin. "OK, see you later," she calls to Carey Welch over the bone saw's scream. She heads for the investigative office, but she is forced to return a few minutes later when a deputy coroner needs her to ask Dr. Rozin a question. Rozin seems busy, so Tracy asks an autopsy tech instead of bothering the doctor. To her mortification, the tech finds this funny. "Dr. Rozin!" he yells. "One of the interns is afraid you're going to bite her!"

Dr. Leon Rozin is in charge of the autopsy room today. The pathologist is seventyish and short enough that lanky Tracy can see the top of his balding head. In his thick Ukrainian accent, Rozin tells one of the techs to stop goofing off and get the next body ready. So the tech moves fast, unceremoniously yanking the homicide victim from the night before, the man who died in the

Hill District, off the gurney and onto one of the autopsy tables. The dead man's head bangs against the steel, a painful clank.

Tracy has read the case file Mike and Tiffani put together last night, and it says he's twenty-seven years old, six feet tall, and 181 pounds. Lying on the table, the homicide is a light-skinned black man, pale-eyed and sporting a well-groomed goatee. The only clue that he's not just sleeping is the dried blood around his mouth and on his orange T-shirt.

A photographer named Mary Ann circles the stainless steel autopsy table, snapping photos of the dead man. Tracy recognizes the little identification tags that Mary Ann places on the body before taking each picture. At college, Tracy attended a slide show put on by a forensic pathologist from Erie, and many of the autopsy slides had these Allegheny County Coroner's Office tags on them. She tells Mary Ann this, and they begin talking.

"In the beginning you remember every case," the photographer tells Tracy. "After a while, you won't remember any of them."

Tracy watches as two autopsy technicians swathed in blue scrubs strip off the homicide's clothing, piling his leather work boots, bright orange T-shirt and black jeans on a nearby gurney. Naked, he has the physique of a sprinter—slim but muscular. His body bears no wrinkles or fat or scars or bruises or cuts or decomposition. No signs of the hard living and age so obvious on the other bodies the interns helped collect the night before. It's hard to believe that this superb body is worthless due to the neat hole in the left side of his chest.

Tracy winces and looks away when a tech slices open the body with a scalpel. With practiced moves, he sweeps the knife down the body, making three long cuts that form a letter Y. The upper branches begin just beneath each shoulder and join just below the sternum. The lower leg of the Y is a single cut down the abdomen to just above the groin. The dark skin gives way to the bright colors of his insides, sere yellow of fat and deep apple-red of muscle. The homicide's fat pad is as thin as a sheet of corrugated cardboard, compared to the inches-thick layer of fat that hung off the overdose's abdomen.

The tech flips down his splash mask, a transparent shield that juts down over his face like a welder's mask, clicks on the electric bone saw and begins severing the homicide's ribs. He lifts the front of the rib cage off the body, baring the inert heart and lungs cached perfectly within the chest.

The organs reveal the exact damage. A dark purple bruise surrounds the hole in the lung, but the worst damage is elsewhere. Rozin reaches into the chest with a scalpel and slices through the aorta, the pulmonary trunk, the superior and inferior vena cava, freeing the heart. Cradling it in his gloved hands, Rozin carries the fist-sized muscle over to the photo table. He points to the damage he wants Mary Ann to photograph—a small tear in the aorta, the great artery through which the heart drives newly oxygenated blood to the rest of the body.

The tech ladles blood from the chest cavity, lots of it from the ruptured aorta. Underneath the sea of blood is the bullet, which did not break the epidermis but left a small external bruise. Rozin pries out the misshapen nugget of metal from the interior of the rear rib cage, taking care not to mar the rifling marks. It is the size of the tip of a child's pinkie finger. Mary Ann photographs it, then places it in a small tan envelope.

"Jacob!" she yells at the autopsy tech. "Here's your bullet. Don't forget. It's right here."

Crime lab technicians will study the .38-caliber bullet to find out what type of gun it was fired from and to try to make an exact match if investigators recover a gun they think was used. In rifles and handguns, spiral grooves run the length of the barrels' interior. These grooves set bullets spinning, which stabilizes their flight, and they also give fired bullets characteristic markings. If a gun is found, crime lab techs will use it to fire a bullet into a water trap and compare it with the one found in the body. This work could help catch a killer, or convict one.

Bullets are no longer dumb chunks of metal. With brand names like Hydra-Shok and Blitz-Action Trauma, the more sophisticated handgun ammunition wreak specific kinds of damage by mushrooming, fragmenting or even exploding inside the body. Even bullets of the same type and caliber can have vastly different effects, depending on the part of the body hit. For instance, most bullet entrance wounds are small and round and the skin instantly tightens around the hole so that it looks smaller than the bullet that just passed through.

However, pressing the gun muzzle against the head in an execution-style shooting will explode the skin in a larger ragged hole because gases from the gun barrel have nowhere to go. The lungs, which have a low density and high degree of elasticity, sustain less cellular damage from a high-velocity bullet than the dense and inelastic liver. A bullet that pierces the body through-and-through without losing its spin is likely to do less damage than one that hits a bone and yaws. Every gunshot wound is different, and an expert can interpret much about the shooting from those distinctions.

The type of firearm used has a major effect as well. A bullet fired from a high-velocity rifle sends out a violent shockwave that can shred surrounding blood vessels, nerves, organs, and sometimes even bones that are not directly hit. A bullet fired from a handgun, however, usually destroys only what is directly in its pathway—the shockwave is not violent enough to do much damage to any tissue it does not directly hit. In other words, if this particular bullet had been an inch to the left or right, it would have missed the aorta and the victim might have lived.

But that's not what happened here. Instead, the bullet punched through his clothes and skin, rubbing raw a ring of flesh around the entrance wound. It tunneled between two ribs, crushing and shredding the tissue directly in its path, including the aorta. At the same time, it flung tissue outward in a shockwave, creating a larger channel of damage. After puncturing the aorta, the bullet traveled easily through the less-dense tissue of the lungs before lodging in the tough skin of the back. Blood began pumping freely into the chest from the hole in the aorta, and the victim's brain began to starve from lack of oxygen. The victim remained conscious for a while, perhaps as much as fifteen seconds, and during that time he managed to run or stumble more than a few steps. As blood spouted from the ruptured aorta, the body's systemic nervous system reacted by releasing adrenaline, which drove the heart to pump faster to make up for the blood loss. Arteries feeding the skin, kidneys, and gastro-intestinal tract tightened so that more blood could be diverted to the heart and brain. But those defensive mechanisms just sent more blood gushing through the tear in the aorta. His famished brain cells began blinking out. Disoriented and weak, he collapsed, forty feet from the spot of the shooting, and died. A simple death, simple as it gets.

Not all homicides are so simple to interpret.

Three weeks earlier, Dr. Bennet Omalu had stood over the autopsy table, studying the sprawled body of a fifty-nine-year-old man wearing the same sweats he died in the day before. Rigor mortis had frozen the dead man in a defensive position, arms bent upward, guarding his head. Like a prizefighter. A flyweight—deputy coroners weighed him in yesterday at 111 pounds.

Bennet fingered the T-shirt stiff with brownish dried blood. The ragged slits in the gray fabric lined up with the wounds underneath, just as they should. For the next few hours, Bennet and his team of two autopsy technicians and a photographer will whirl around the autopsy table. The pathologist will scrutinize wounds, manipulate broken bones, section organs, and sometimes even sniff the air for the distinctly sweet smell of alcohol-soaked organs. Techs do most of the physical labor—stripping the body, cleaning and cutting it open, removing the organs, drawing body fluids, and sewing the corpse back together with a thick curved needle and heavy twine. The photographer will provide a complete visual record of each autopsied body and its injuries. Photos may be needed if laboratory work brings new facts to light. By the time the case goes to trial, the body will be long gone, buried or incinerated. Every bit of evidence that can be gathered must be gathered now, even if the odds of coming up with something are unlikely.

The photographer on this case, Lisa Leon, began working at the coroner's office last September. Before that she was a wedding photographer. She likes her new job much better. Instead of making the same ho-hum pictures over and over—the vows at the altar, the family groupings, the first kiss—she sees something new every day here.

"Do we know why this guy's dead?" she asked Bennet.

"Yeah," the pathologist said, deadpan. "I killed him."

In fact, someone had already confessed to killing the man on the table. This was documented in the printout on Bennet's clipboard, the case "story" entered into the computer by the deputy coroners who picked up the body. According to the story, an emergency call the day before alerted paramedics to a fight at the victim's house in Wilkinsburg, a rough suburb just east of the city. The medics followed a trail of blood from the front door to the living room to find the victim lying face-up, hands defensively upturned, among overturned tables and chairs, broken glass and lamps. The deputy coroners were still investigating the death scene when they got the report that a man had just walked into a police station and confessed to the homicide.

So they had a killer, but as Bennet took an initial look at the body, the cause of death was unclear. The T-shirt and sheets in the nearby body bag were soaked with blood, though it was hard to say if the wounds to the torso were enough to cause the man to bleed out and die. The small man had a narrow-cut mustache and his hard bald head was battered and cut, his right eye caved in. His left eye was slightly open. A brown electric cord with a plug on the end was tangled in the man's shirt, and the deputy coroners thought he'd been choked.

Bennet looked at the red cloth shorts that had slipped above the waistband of the dead man's green nylon sweatpants. He needed to describe them for his records, but he was not sure what to call them. After five years in the United States, he was still learning new terms.

"These are boxers?" he asked Patti Kurzawski, one of two autopsy technicians who was assisting him with this case.

"No, these aren't boxer shorts, these are sweat shorts," Patti said.

"Sweatshirts?" Bennet asked.

"Sweat *shorts*," Patti said.

Bennet jotted this down. He didn't mind asking questions, showing ignorance. He knew he had a lot to learn yet, both about American slang and pathology. Growing up in Nigeria, Bennet had wanted to be a jet pilot—he wanted action. He went into medicine on his father's advice, but he didn't like working with patients. What he liked was the challenge of diagnosis, the intellectual challenge—a mystery to solve. Autopsies gave him that, and so did talking to cops and family members, tracking down a cause of death.

He found it difficult to get the words in an autopsy report just right, and not only because English was not his native tongue. The language of an autopsy report, he had found, must achieve a fine balance. The words must be precise and accurate, yet broad enough so that the report's conclusions are not likely to be challenged. This kind of semantic mincing was not natural to him. Bennet preferred bluntness.

He was also impatient—if techs were slowing him down, he'd bark half-jokingly at them to hurry up. As soon as the mystery was solved, the cause of death revealed, the job became routine for him, a careful documentation of facts, a job nothing like flying a jet.

"Dr. O., do you want a neutron?" Patti called out. "Do I want what?" he asked.

"Do you want a neutron test done on the hands?" Patti repeated. A neutron test, or atomic absorption test, would detect whether or not the victim fired a gun recently.

"Yes, please," Bennet said, sounding as if he thought Patti should have known he wanted one.

"Well, it was a stabbing, they said, but if you want it . . ." she said.

Bennet didn't believe a gun was involved, but he wanted to be sure. If he didn't, the defendant could claim self-defense, say the victim shot at him.

Paper bags covered the man's hands like boxing gloves. Patti removed rubber bands and slid the bags off. Deputy coroners had bagged the hands at the scene the day before, a routine precaution in homicide cases. Hands bear evidence—blood, skin, hair—that often can be dislodged in transport. Deputy coroners use paper instead of plastic, because still-warm hands will produce condensation inside a plastic bag, and the dampness could destroy evidence such as gunshot residue.

Patti stopped chewing her gum momentarily to concentrate on swabbing the hands for gunshot residue. Patti is the chief autopsy technician, which means she supervises the other five techs, orders supplies, and schedules shifts. And every two or three weeks, she climbs up on the photographer's ladder, unhooks the eight spider plants that hang around the room, lines them up on one of the autopsy tables and drenches them from a rubber hose. The others don't notice the spider plants until watering time, but Patti frets about their stringiness and pale hue, due most likely to the room's lack of sunlight. She calls them her babies.

The spider plants filter toxins from the air and combat the vinegary stink of formalin. The autopsy room always smells, but the smell changes from day to day, body to body. If they have a stinker, the roadkill stench can drift down the hallway, through the investigative office, and into the lobby where cops and lawyers and grieving families come in. A bad stinker can send fumes all the way up the broad marble staircase to the administrative offices on the second floor or even the inquest courtroom on the third floor. On days when there's no stinker, the odor is different, subtler, an old-linen scent of elderly neglect or the uneasy sweat-smell of violence or a hospital antiseptic whiff of illness. And always there is the acridity of formalin and the industrial-strength bouquet of antibacterial cleaner. Patti's spider plants help only so much.

A skinny woman with short auburn hair and sharp, squinty eyes, Patti has worked in this room for twenty-six years—long enough that new pathologists often will take her advice on unusual cases. Originally she studied to become a medical assistant, but quickly found that she couldn't handle the job. She passed out during a film on face-lifting surgery. She passed out during a tour of the blood bank. She even passed out when her daughter cut her finger.

But when Patti tried the coroner's office, she was fine. Dead bodies she could handle—for them, the pain was over. Live people were another matter. When families used to come back to the autopsy room to identify bodies, she would stand there and cry with them. She's relieved that they now view the bodies in another room. The dead are OK; the still-suffering give her problems.

Patti and the other autopsy tech, Sis Comer, began pulling off the homicide victim's clothing and placing the articles on stretchers lined with paper sheets.

Two white socks on each skinny foot. Sweatpants. Shorts. The man's legs were stick thin. Bennet ran his fingers over the sweatpants and shorts, studying every inch of fabric for anything out of the ordinary. Nothing.

Sis began wrestling off the dead man's T-shirt. "Holy cow," she exclaimed after pulling it up over his gaunt torso.

Working on another body across the room, another tech called: "Holy cow, what?"

Sis was studying a gaping vertical stab wound in the center of the man's belly, just beneath the ribs. It was a vicious cut. "They did a liver stick on him right down the middle," she said.

Other techs chuckled.

Clothed, the man had looked slim. Naked, he was gaunt, webbed with wiry muscle, a cardboard cutout of a real man. The metal support on the table beneath him thrust out his bantam chest. Corpses must be naked for autopsy. This seems like common sense, but not everybody realizes it. Sis's husband one day asked her about this—it had just never entered his mind that his wife worked with naked bodies. He never visits her at the coroner's office and rarely asks her about her day. In fact, he won't even call her at work anymore, not since the day she told him that the buzzing sound he was hearing over the phone was a bone saw, one of the techs popping a skull.

Bennet noted the abdominal wound; despite its surface size, it didn't look that deep or bloody. There was a deep muscle gash on the shoulder and smaller wounds scattered around the chest.

Sis untangled the electric cord from the man's shirt. Bennet took a look. "This was not wrapped around his neck, it was just laying around his shirt," she told him.

Bennet detected no choke marks on the man's neck. The deputy coroners the day before saw the placement of the cord and assumed it was used to strangle the man. Now it appeared not to have been a weapon, an important reversal. If the dead man had been beaten, stabbed, *and* choked, that might lead to different assumptions in court than if he were just beaten and stabbed.

For instance, a prosecutor could argue that an additional weapon shows malicious intent, that it wasn't an accident. Bennet and Sis stretched the cord along the table, then measured its length with a tape measure.

Lisa was using a Polaroid now for the "dirty shots," the photos that showed the blood and appearance of the wounds before they cleaned him up. She will photograph the body in layers—with clothes, then naked, then free of blood and grime. She pulled out the photos and put them on the nearby stretcher to develop next to the dead man's shorts. Lisa orbited the autopsy table, shooting from every angle. Tight shots of the individual chest wounds, the damaged eye socket, the lacerations around the head. She climbed a short metal ladder mounted on wheels to get a bird's-eye shot of the upper body, then moved it over to get the lower body. Coroner's photos are not particularly artistic, but they must be technically sound and crisp, and this requires expertise. While shooting, Lisa twisted into awkward positions so the flash would not shadow a laceration or bruise. It's an athletic task, photographing an autopsy without holding up the process, full of thigh lunges and crouching and stair climbing.

Sis propped a box of soapy water on the man's spindly thighs and began washing him down with a sponge. Tinged red with blood, the water swirled toward a basin at the end of the table, running constantly during the autopsy. Sis scrubbed his skinny arms and shoulders; the blood was clotted on hard. Lisa waited for Sis to towel off the corpse before taking the clean shots so that no glare would bounce off the sheen of water on the skin and obscure part of the photo.

Sis pulled on the man's arm to straighten it out, and his ropy biceps bulged out in resistance. In most corpses, rigor mortis sets in after about four hours, peaks in ten hours or so, then fades away after thirty-six hours. This is just a coroner's rule of thumb, however, and not an accurate time-of-death gauge. Cold weather may slow the process, and vigorous activity before death (such as fighting off a killer) may speed it up. Muscles contain an energy-giving chemical called adenosine triphosphate that helps them contract and relax.

The chemical gradually depletes after death and, without it, the muscles lock into place, first the small stringy sinews of the eyelids, face, and neck and then the larger ones in the arms, torso, and thighs. Then, as the muscle cells begin to break down and decompose, rigor fades away.

Decomposition had not yet drained the strength from this man's hard musculature. He had been killed a little more than twenty-four hours ago, so he probably had a few more hours of stiffness left. For a moment, Sis and the dead man were locked in an arm-wrestle. "Whoa, is he in rigor," she grunted. "Jeeze."

When the body was ready, Bennet pulled on a splash mask and began the methodical process of measuring each cut and bruise on the body. He marked the locations on a sheet of paper that showed right- and left-side profiles.

The head alone bore dozens of marks of violence. To the untrained eye, the broken-skin wounds looked similar, but Bennet could see that more than one weapon had been used. Some of the marks were simple slices that looked like they had been caused by a knife. Pathologists have exhaustively documented the differences between wounds from single-bladed knives, double-bladed knives, serrated-blade knives, knives with hilts, ice picks, forks, pencils, broken cue sticks, scissors, and broken bottles. A Phillips-head screwdriver stabbing is particularly easy to identify—an X marks the entry wound.

Forensic pathologists also can tell the approximate age of bruises from their coloring—from fresh purple-black to older yellow-green. They can also tell whether a wound happened before or after death. Live tissue reacts to damage by bleeding; within an hour, the body sends white cells to the area to help it heal. Dead tissue doesn't swell or bruise, and cuts are pale yellow and show little bleeding.

In this stabbing case, other spots where the skin was split bore radiating lacerations, which indicated that a blunt-force instrument had been used, not a cutting edge. From the size and shape, Bennet was thinking it might have been a hammer. A picture of the attack was emerging.

On the surface, the worst injuries to the body were a deep slice on the shoulder and the abdominal wound. On the head, the worst injury was the crushed right eye. The eye was slashed and the orbital cavity caved inward. Because the eye was sliced as well as crushed, Bennet believed a forceful knife thrust had caused this fracture. The lens of the eye had come out and was lying on the man's eyelid. The once-crystalline scrap of tissue that bent and focused light onto the retina was yellowish, opaque, and jellylike. Bennet picked it up and dabbed it onto the chest of his sea-green scrubs for safekeeping. It stuck there while he moved around the body, like a yellow diamond lapel pin.

Bennet had to record every mark on the homicide victim before they could open the body or take more photographs. As he moved slowly down the body, most of the staffers had retreated to the autopsy lounge, where Lisa had left a paperback copy of *From Potter's Field*, a Patricia Cornwell thriller from the series about a medical examiner in Virginia. A solitary tech mopped the floor on the other side of the room.

This part of the case, the routine documentation of wounds, bored Bennet. It got him no closer to the core of the mystery. When he got to the torso, Bennet used a device that looked like an extra-long swizzle stick to probe inside the stab wounds and measure the depth and angle the blade had taken. He could also tell the angle of some of the lacerating blows because the tissue on the side the blow was coming from was abraded and beveled.

The photographer wandered back in, and Bennet groaned: "The murderer did this to make my life miserable, to punish me."

"And me," Lisa said.

Bennet pointed to a cut on the back of the forearm. "That is a defense wound," he told the photographer. "Did you take it?"

Lisa was disbelieving. She had shot the hands already and did not see anything. "Where?"

Just like the hands, any wounds on the forearms, especially the backs of the forearms, should be documented as defense wounds, Bennet explained to her. He demonstrated, crouching as if defending himself from a blow and raising his arms to shield his body and head to show how his forearms would bear the brunt of an attack.

Sis returned to the autopsy room just in time to flip the body for Bennet. This was usually a two-person job, but Sis told Patti that she needed no help. "He's so skinny," she murmured, grabbing an arm and bracing her other hand against his hip. He flopped over with a thump, revealing flat buttocks and a constellation of cuts on his back. Most of the wounds looked minor, but the presence of defense wounds and back lacerations would strengthen the prosecution's case.

For Bennet, the viciousness of the attack made no sense. "If you want to kill someone, why would you stab someone fifty-four times?" he said.

"We gotta send out a memo to these murderers—stab 'em one time, that's all it takes, right through the heart," one of the techs replied. "I'm sure that one in the chest killed him anyhow."

The tech was talking about a cut on the upper back. It was less showy on the surface than the gaping abdominal wound on the other side, but Bennet agreed it may have been the fatal wound because of its depth and placement. They would know when they cut him open whether the blade had perforated the rib cage and done damage to the heart or arteries or lungs. On the other hand, the cause of death might not have been the stab wounds at all. It might have been blunt force trauma to the head. Turning the man over had revealed another hammer blow to the back of his head.

By the time Bennet had documented every exterior wound, more than two hours had passed since the victim had been pulled onto the autopsy table. It was almost noon, and Bennet still didn't know how the man had died.

"Doc, can I open him now?" Patti asked.

"Yeah, sure," Bennet said.

Until the body and the skull were cut open and Bennet could study the internal damage, he had little to do. He hovered as Patti and Sis flipped the body face-up again. He wondered about the larger questions of the case, how it all fit together. One thing puzzled him: what had the killer used as the blunt-force instrument? The deputy coroner's story mentioned only knife wounds. If the police didn't know about the blunt-force instrument, they should begin looking for it.

"Do we know if the killer used a hammer?" he asked.

"We can call the detectives and ask them," Sis said.

Bennet agreed, and Sis called on the autopsy-room phone. While she was waiting for an answer, Patti made the Y-shaped incision from the man's chest to stomach. Bennet instructed her to cut around the large wound in the man's abdomen to preserve the walls of the cut in case he needed to examine it again. "What was the motive for this?" Bennet asked Patti.

Patti didn't understand. "Pardon me?" she asked.

"The motive, the motive?" Bennet said. The word sounded like *mo-TIF*.

"I still don't know what you're saying," Patti said. "The motive for the guy's stabbing," Bennet repeated. "Oh, the motive," Patti said.

"The motive," Bennet said, emulating her pronunciation, softening the word to *MO-div*.

"I don't know," Patti said, peeling back the victim's thin flap of chest and abdominal skin. Now Bennet could see which wounds did damage. A relatively small surface cut near the left nipple had caused a good deal of bleeding inside the skin. But what mattered most was what had happened inside the rib cage, where the vital organs were cached, the lungs and the heart. Like the rest of the body, those organs provide a biographical record of sorts. An enlarged heart may be due to clogged arteries that force the pumping muscle to work harder and grow. Tarry lungs usually belong to smokers—although older Pittsburghers also tend to have black lungs, a remnant of the days when steel mills poured smoke into the air and businessmen brought an extra white shirt to work downtown because the first one was stained with soot by noon.

Sis hung up the phone after talking to the detective on the case. "As far as they know, the suspect says he used only a knife and a lamp," she said.

"A lamp," Bennet repeated. A heavy lamp base would account for the blunt force blows. It might also have explained the electric cord tangled in the clothing. Bennet's picture of a combined knife and blunt-force instrument attack was proving to be correct.

"There are other tools there at the house—a hammer and screwdrivers—but the suspect said he used a lamp on him, so that's probably what it is," Sis said.

Patti severed each rib with shears and then lifted off the chest plate, exposing the heart, lungs, trachea, aorta, and esophagus. Immediately the damage was clear. The right side of the chest cavity looked fine; the left was awash in blood, maybe thirty cubic centimeters' worth. Patti used a large syringe to extract a sample of the chest blood and squirt it into a tube. When she lifted out the left lung, Bennet could see the ragged wound in the back of the slippery purple organ.

So the knife had slipped through the ribs of the back. That cut had done more damage than all the other bodily stab wounds, the gaping stomach wound, the slash on the shoulder muscle, the bloody cut near the left nipple. Dozens of slashes, and the unassuming cut in the back was the one that had caught a vital organ, the lung. It could have been what killed him. It was still hard to say if he had bled out. The head trauma could have gotten him first. Once again, cutting him open, this time the head, could provide a final answer.

The bug zapper in the corner snapped, and Lisa said: "Got one."

Sis slid a big syringe into the dead man's heart, extracted blood and squirted it into a labeled test tube. She drew urine from the bladder and bile from the liver and put them in different tubes. The toxicology lab would later test these fluids along with fluid drawn earlier from the eyes.

Sis swiftly cut away the abdominal organs, the stomach, intestinal tract, liver, spleen, kidneys, and gall bladder. Despite the big abdominal wound that first had caught her eye, the one she earlier had compared to a liver probe, there was no damage there, no blood. She moved up to the head and prepared to open it.

Having documented every wound, Bennet turned to the basin along the wall and began to dissect the organs Sis had removed. With a long knife, Bennet sliced them in half like a cantaloupe, then nipped off small sections with a scalpel. He plopped one cut of each organ in a large jar of formalin; another went in a small jar of the fixative. The formalin—a mixture of formaldehyde and water—will "fix" the specimens, preserving them so they can be retrieved and studied indefinitely. (Recently, the doctors decided the office's formalin needed more calcium, so the autopsy techs began collecting eggshells from the restaurant next door and crushing them up in the solution.)

The large jar would be stored away in the basement for four or more years, just in case something came up about the case and more tests needed to be run. The small jar would go to the histology lab, where the organ sections would be dyed and put on slides for microscopic scrutiny.

Just as Sis was preparing to slice open the damaged and hairless scalp, two of the office's four pathologists walked in: Dr. Abdul Shakir and Dr. Leon Rozin. Both men had supervised Bennet during his fellowship. Shakir was wearing a suit and tie; he had testified in court that morning. Rozin wore the usual long white coat. The following conversation was a linguist's dream—three men discussing a complex death case in three unrelated accents: Iraqi, Ukrainian, and Nigerian. The mixture of articulations bouncing around the autopsy room really gets complex when Jacob, the excitable Polish autopsy tech, is involved, but he was not around at the moment. All four of the office's pathologists (not including Wecht) come from other countries; Dr. Shaun Ladham is Canadian. Wecht, the son of Jewish immigrants from Lithuania and Ukraine, was born in a coal patch south of Pittsburgh.

There is a stereotype of the forensic pathologist as a foreigner, relegated to this area of medicine because he or she did not attend medical school in the United States. In fact, in recent decades a third to a half of all pathology residents in the United States have been graduates of foreign medical schools, which are generally considered inferior to those in the United States. Too few American medical school students view the field as attractive, in part because of the lack of patient contact.

Shakir and Rozin exchanged greetings with the autopsy staffers, and Bennet explained the case, listing the major injuries, the head trauma, and the stab wound in the back. His gloved hands bloody from the organ dissection, Bennet's voice grew formalistic, adopting a stand-and-deliver tone likely developed through years of presenting patients in medical school.

Serendipitously, Sis was just now peeling back the scalp, which was white underneath and perforated with cuts and splits in the skin. The surface of the skull was shiny and smooth and one of its sutures was cracked open, leaving a centimeter-wide gap. "There's a fracture on the head, too," she added.

"So this guy died most probably of the blunt force trauma of the head?" Shakir asked Bennet.

"There's nothing in his abdomen, no blood?" Rozin pressed.

"No, but there's blood in the left chest cavity," Bennet said.

Sis chipped in: "The blow to the eye probably caused this fracture here. He hit him with a lamp."

Bennet summed up: "He most likely died from the blow that caused the depressed fracture on the right frontal bone and the deep laceration and contusion of the right upper eyelid."

"According to the news, the guy who did it said he did it in self-defense," Shakir said. "I have defense wounds," Bennet said.

"But what was the reason, though?" Sis asked. "Drugs? Girlfriend? Money? Sexual crime?"

"I don't know," Shakir said. Like everyone else, the coroner's office staffers will find out more about the case in a couple of weeks, when the inquest is held in the courtroom two floors up. Motive isn't their concern. Forensic pathologists say it is better to distance yourself from police theories about a killing and just let yourself be guided by the facts of the autopsy.

As the doctors conferred, Sis turned on the bone saw, which was plugged in underneath the autopsy table, and started cutting open the skull. The saw's vibrating blade carved through bone without damaging surrounding soft tissue, such as the brain. Sis began the cut near the top of the head and gradually made a sweatband-sized circle in the skull. She cut a notch on one side so it would be easy to refit the skullcap and pull the scalp back over the now-hollow cranium. The damage from the autopsy would not be noticeable—the family could even have an open-casket funeral if the wounds from the attack weren't so visible. The bone saw stopped with a chunking sound, and Sis dropped it to the tile floor with a clank. She pried open the skull cap with a metal claw tool, then yanked it off and placed it on the table. Rozin prodded her left biceps and raised his eyebrows, impressed.

Sis slid her hand between brain and inner skull, searching for the spinal cord at the base. She poked her scalpel into the crevice, sliced across the cord and lifted out the gray bundle of nerve connections in both hands. She handed the brain to Lisa, who cradled it in two gloved hands so Rozin and Shakir could gather around and poke at it, looking for telltale swelling or bruising. The damage was difficult for the untrained eye to see, but the pathologists could see that the patterned crevices in the brain surface were not as deep as they should have been. They showed Lisa what parts to photograph. She placed the brain on the photography table and stuck on it tiny white paper arrows that pointed to the damage. Before snapping pictures, she stripped off her gloves so she wouldn't get brain matter on the camera.

Now Rozin and Shakir were convinced that the brain damage was the deadly culprit Bennet had been searching for. When Sis pointed out the amount of blood on the sheets in the body bag, Shakir said that he thinks that blood had come from the head wounds, not the lung.

Rozin ended the guesswork phase of the case with a single statement: "I would say it is sharp and blunt-force trauma because we don't know how much blood he lost in the chest wound." Rozin was certain the brain injuries would have killed the man; he was not certain about the deadliness of the lung wound. Therefore, the brain injuries would take the blame.

"You can write it as sharp and blunt, or blunt and sharp-force," Rozin explained.

"What about the stab wound to the lung?" Bennet asked.

Rozin told Bennet to write up the lung injury as an additional factor in the death. Shakir began explaining exactly how Bennet should write the report.

Bennet nodded, his face expressionless.

Much work remained. He had to write up the case, get the wording just right—exact yet fuzzy enough to give him room to move. In a matter of days, coroner's officials would hold an inquest, hear testimony, and decide whether or not to send the case to trial as a homicide.

But for Bennet, the mystery was over. Over, but not completely solved. Why had the dead man's heart stopped beating? Had it run out of blood? Or had the brain stopped telling it to beat? Bennet couldn't say for sure. But the fun part was over.

That was three weeks ago. Today, the cause of death is obvious: a bullet-punctured aorta.

As Tracy watches, an autopsy tech rolls the young homicide victim into the cooler. But the bodies keep coming: the cornea donor, the old lady who lived next to the monastery, a big fat man. *At first you remember every case . . . then you don't remember any of them.* Tracy can't believe she'll forget any of the cases. She's not sure she wants to.

Tracy tries to pay attention, but she keeps looking away during the bad parts. Her jaw drops when a tech lifts out the fat man's sausagelike mass of intestines. A tech pokes around with a syringe for a few moments before hitting the right spot and drawing the rich red liquid into a vial. A scalpel cleaves the chest tattoo of the fat man. The debate is renewed concerning whether the cornea donor had been circumcised. (Sis confirms that he has been but the job was shoddy.) The worst thing is the crunching sound of the bone saw. Tracy thinks it will be at least a couple of weeks before she can watch someone pop a skull.

Most people feel some anxiety around dead bodies. Women are more likely to react negatively to cadavers, according to surveys of medical students undergoing autopsy and dissection training. Some medical students felt sick or even fainted during the procedures; afterward, some suffered nightmares or swore off meat. Like Tracy, many couldn't grasp the idea that the corpses felt no pain, and they found cutting around the head and face particularly difficult to do. Researchers theorize that people can't fully grasp the concept of their own mortality, so they find it hard to accept that the bodies in front of them are truly dead, beyond pain.

But the raw shock of death seemed to fade quickly for medical students. Often, the anticipation of cutting open a dead body proved to be worse than the reality. Conditioned by movies and popular culture, the students expected their confrontations with dead bodies to be more dramatic than they turned out to be. Opened, the bodies became anatomy textbooks. Cognition took over. Body parts had to be learned, procedures mastered. A few days into dissection, the cadavers had lost their immediate impact. But being around death seems to have a subtle long-term effect. One 1994 study showed that, as a set of medical students grew accustomed to working with cadavers, they grew more callous in response to hypothetical questions involving death and accidents.

Carey Welch feels more at home than Tracy in the autopsy room. Sensing her ease, the techs have already begun to recruit her for small tasks—taking organ weights and handling equipment they don't want to get blood on. As she jots down organ weights, she sits on a desk—never mind germs—and crosses her tired legs. Carey's mother picked her up at the office around 10:00 p.m. last night, and she came back in early this morning.

Despite her fatigue, Carey is pleased to be here. So far, the autopsy experience has been as intriguing as the surgical documentaries she loves watching on television. The autopsies resemble surgical procedures in some ways: The light box on the wall, for example, where the pathologists hold up X-ray images, bodies and bones that look like cumulus clouds marred by the harsh white spot of a bullet. The gear that the pathologist and the techs are wearing. Two sets of latex gloves, surgical masks, white plastic sleeve protectors, and white plastic aprons over their surgical scrubs. Unlike surgery, however, all this gear is designed to protect the people performing the operation, not the body on the table. Pathologists have caught streptococcal infections, hepatitis, and tuberculosis from bodies, not to mention lice and poison ivy; before penicillin a few died from infections. Bodies considered high-risk—those of prostitutes, suspected AIDS sufferers, hemophiliacs—are labeled as such. Like all of the coroner's employees, the interns were asked to get tested for tuberculosis and vaccinated for hepatitis before starting at the office.

Other differences between autopsy and surgery are also apparent. Although the techs take care not to deface body parts that may be on view during the funeral, they eviscerate the bodies with a brutal quickness, crunching ribs with big shears and saws, quickly cutting free the organs. They don't cauterize or tie blood vessels. The damage doesn't matter. These bodies won't heal.

And that's the other big difference between autopsy and surgery. In surgery, hearts throb, lungs heave. There are intravenous lines, anesthesia, breathing and pulse monitors. Here, the bodies are still, organs drained of vitality and color. Nobody is in pain. Any urgency surrounding the case involves the people who are still alive and looking for answers: the cops, family members, the news media. In surgery, blood is everywhere, pumping and jetting, a constant concern. In the autopsy room, there is plenty of blood, but it is thickening and inert. It doesn't squirt—it drains passively.

Despite her own interest, Carey realizes Tracy is having a hard time. When a tech calls the interns over to show them the placement of the abdominal organs, Carey strokes Tracy's hair sympathetically.

"You all right?" she asks.

Tracy nods. But a few moments later, she retreats once again to the investigative office, escaping the sights and smells and sounds of the autopsy room. Tracy will soon find out that the autopsy room is a haven compared to the place they call the crying room.

THREE

THE CRYING ROOM

The investigative office is packed with people; Tracy has to squeeze in. Mary Ann, the photographer, and all three day-shift deputy coroners are hanging around, no calls right now. Tracy met everybody when she started the shift at 7:00 a.m.

No sooner had Tracy sat down than the coroner's office receptionist pokes her head into the investigative office and says that the family of a deceased person just came in, the mother and four other people. They're in the hallway. The receptionist says the family's name and the name of the dead man.

Jimmy, the senior deputy on day-shift duty today, shrugs. "Who's that?"

Another deputy says, "That's the name of the homicide."

Jimmy looks pained and flustered. Deputy coroners hate this part of the job—when families come into the office, often uninvited and distraught and demanding to see their children, parents, spouses. But it happens often.

"Do we have a photo?" Jimmy asks.

"I don't know," another deputy says. "I need to read the case story."

Jimmy says he's already printing it out. Mary Ann says that they just finished the homicide autopsy—the victim is bagged and already back in the cooler. Jimmy grabs a clipboard out of a filing cabinet and clips the printout of the case story to it. Another deputy reads it. The dead man's aunt recognized him at the scene, so they already have a positive ID.

"Since he's already been identified, why are they here?" one deputy frets.

"Well . . . they're here," Jimmy says with finality.

Everybody knows exactly why the mother is here. She's here for the same reason mothers always come to the coroner's office. They don't quite believe their sons are dead, and they hope that coming here will help them fathom what happened. And maybe, just maybe, they'll find out that someone made a glorious mistake, that in the dim light of the housing project courtyard last night, her son's aunt *thought* the dead man was her nephew, but she was *wrong*, he was a stranger, a total stranger.

The receptionist goes back to the family in the entrance hall. Tracy peeks out there. Two men and three women follow the receptionist into a hallway behind the reception desk.

Mary Ann and another deputy go to the cooler, where they pull out the homicide's gurney and halfway unzip the body bag. Blood is visible where the dead man's skull was sliced open, so Mary Ann covers the top of his head with plastic. She stands on a chair above the gurney and shoots two Polaroids.

The other deputy zips the body bag back up, then takes off her latex gloves and looks at the Polaroids. They're gray and cloudy, still developing. Impatiently, she fans them in the air, trying to hurry the development, knowing the family is waiting. The image gradually surfaces and brightens, revealing the upper body of the very dead-looking man, swaddled in a body bag on the gurney, his eyes slightly open.

But there's one problem. The tops of the Y cut on the man's upper chest are showing. The deputy covers the damage with two strips of tape, goes back to the investigative office and gives the photo to Jimmy, who clips it onto the clipboard along with the case story. Then he heads into the hallway behind the reception desk to talk to the family.

For decades, bodies have been identified in this part of the coroner's office. When the building was first built almost a century ago, a marble-walled chapel towered over the space where the hallway now runs. The dead lay on cool marble slabs in a majestic room with sixty-foot arching walls, washed by the tinted light coming through thirteen massive stained-glass windows. Back then, the Allegheny County Mortuary, as the coroner's office building was known, was open to the public twenty-four hours a day. Fewer people carried identification in those days, and the office lacked the technology to identify them, so many unidentified, embalmed bodies lay in the chapel until someone claimed them or the county cremated them after weeks or months had passed. Often the only way to find out whether a relative was missing, drunk, or dead was to visit the hospitals, bars, and the coroner's chapel in person. (This still happens, mostly over the phone. Lately, a woman has called the coroner's office almost every evening, asking if there are any new unidentified bodies. She tells the deputy coroners that she's trying to find her daughter's missing boyfriend.) Later, banks of glass-topped coolers were built, running down both long walls of the chapel and lit by decorative sconces on the marble walls above. The bodies lay uncovered on gurneys that were tilted so that visitors could see them easily through the glass.

Years ago, young couples in tuxedos and ball gowns often mingled with the dead in a local rite of passage. After proms or graduations, groups of teenagers visited the chapel to pay their respects to the dead, the boys trying to look stoic, the shrieks of the girls echoing in the high-vaulted room. Nobody knows how this custom got its start, but older Pittsburghers say the boys proposed touring the coroner's chapel in hopes that their petrified dates would need comforting afterward. The tradition ended in 1966, when Dr. William R. Hunt was elected head of the coroner's office and ended the public display of dead bodies as part of his reform movement to make the office more scientific. "Ninety percent of the people who go in there do it out of pure idle curiosity and I think it's ghoulish as hell," Hunt told the *Pittsburgh Post-Gazette* that year. (Coincidentally, Dr. Cyril Wecht, Hunt's partner in revolutionizing the coroner's office, has boyhood memories of ducking into the chapel himself to check out the dead folks.)

A few years later, Hunt built the hallway and offices behind the reception desk. But the chapel still stands above. If you lift a panel in the hallway ceiling and look up through the crack, you can see the white walls stretching upward. Daylight glows dimly through the stained-glass windows above, filthy and cobwebbed from years of obscurity. Two years earlier, Wecht proposed building a second floor of offices within the chapel, saying the plan would give the coroner's office some much-needed space and also take advantage of the elegant architecture. The plan has not been realized.

As the morgue modernized in the 1970s, the coroner's office began searching more diligently for next of kin. One now retired deputy coroner, Mary Pacacha, was partly responsible for that change. Although she had no official obligation to do so, Pacacha began hunting for survivors on her cases. She combed pockets and homes, looking for scraps of paper with telephone numbers to call. She telephoned neighbors, queried delivery people and placed "survivors sought" notices in the local newspapers. She sent the fingerprints of unidentified bodies to federal and local law enforcement agencies in case the dead person had served in the military or had a criminal record. (Nowadays, there is so much DNA hype that people often ask why the coroner's office can't identify remains by examining genetic material. Because, the deputy coroners explain patiently, what would they compare the results to? The FBI Laboratory does operate a national database that contains 1.4 million DNA profiles of convicted offenders, but it's a very long shot that the remains in Pittsburgh will be among them. The database is used to match DNA found at crime scenes, not DNA from remains.)

These days, deputy coroners routinely call physicians, social workers, state agencies, and homeless shelters to track down survivors. Finding a survivor is usually attributable to brute persistence and luck, not masterly detective skills. Sometimes it comes down to simply calling everyone in the telephone book with the same last name, asking over and over if they know the deceased, as Tiffani did a couple weeks ago after an old woman died alone on the South Side. So many people said they didn't know the woman that when one said the dead woman was a cousin, Tiffani was struck mute for a moment. She gathered her thoughts, cleared her throat and said: "I'm sorry to inform you—she was found dead."

In a society that prefers euphemisms for the word "dead," some novice deputy coroners have a hard time using the word when informing someone that a child or spouse or parent has died. It seems too severe a word. But clarity is crucial, according to a death notification expert who lectured at the coroner's office a few weeks earlier.

Mary Cimador, a registered nurse and instructor at a local community college, spoke to the deputy coroners as part of a continuing education program. How a deputy coroner handles the death notification can affect how smoothly the relative eases into the grief process. This is a moment that the relative will remember always, Cimador reminded the deputies. It can also help relatives cope with the concept of the autopsy. Some groups balk at autopsies on religious grounds. Hmongs, recent arrivals from Asia, believe that mutilation after death prevents the dead person's spirit from passing to the next life. Orthodox Jews, a significant population in Pittsburgh, forbid autopsy except in situations in which an autopsy may save another life, such as when the death is believed to be a result of homicide or a deadly virus.

Although immediate reactions to death vary from culture to culture and person to person, many people feel an immediate shock and bewilderment. For thirty seconds or so, they may feel like they cannot breathe. They may hyperventilate or even have a heart attack. To restore breathing patterns, Cimador said, tell survivors to cup their hands over their mouths and noses so that they re-breathe carbon dioxide, triggering a return to normal breathing. Some survivors may get angry and even throw a punch at the bearer of the news, Cimador said. (Deputy coroners at the seminar nodded grimly at this; many have been attacked in that situation.)

"Passed away" is not the only cliché to avoid, Cimador said. Statements such as "It was God's will" or "You must be strong for the children" are often unhelpful.

"Don't say, 'I know just how you feel.' No, you really don't—you're not in that person's shoes at that time," Cimador told the deputy coroners. "Don't say, 'Time heals all wounds.' Some parents never get over the death of a child, so you can't make that statement. Don't say, 'Things will get better.' Things may or may not get better, you don't know."

Instead, Cimador advised, say, "I'm sorry for your loss," or "I know this must be painful." And provide information. Collect details about the death beforehand. Typically, people want to understand exactly what happened.

Make death notifications in person, Cimador urged, not over the telephone. Show interest through body language. Make eye contact. Hold your head straight toward the other person. Sit down if the other person is seated, but sit forward, don't lean back, don't cross your arms or legs, make sure your hands and feet are comfortably at rest. Deliver the news in doses. (I need to speak to you about your son. . . . He was involved in a shooting. . . . I'm sorry, but he has died.)

The deputy coroners at the seminar thought many of Cimador's suggestions were helpful, but others were impractical. The deputies are often running from one case to another and don't have much time to spend with survivors. And they often must break the news over the telephone, because sometimes police will track down a next of kin and tell them nothing more than to call the coroner's office. Police have been known to just leave a handwritten note with a phone number on the door of a survivor's home: *Call the coroner's office.*

After the next of kin has made funeral arrangements and the autopsy is complete, the next step is releasing the body. Funeral home workers back their hearses up to the garage doors at the rear of the building, where deputy coroners meet them with the body. After double-checking the photo and identification bracelet and exchanging paperwork, they pull the body bag onto the funeral home gurney and shove it into the hearse. (Deputy coroners chuckle about the director of a discount funeral home who drives a beat-up pickup truck, no hearse. He simply slides the bodies into the open truck bed and drives off. "What's he do if it starts raining?" one deputy wondered aloud.)

When foreigners die in Pittsburgh, it's not as easy. A few weeks ago, when the German businessman fell down the stairs and died, it fell to a deputy coroner named Ed Strimlan to track down a next of kin. In this case, the next of kin was the dead man's wife in Ratingen, Germany. Pennsylvania falls within the jurisdiction of the German consulate in New York City, so Ed dialed that office in the United Nations Plaza and got a woman with a slight German accent.

Ed introduced himself and said: "A gentleman was just found passed away here at 1:00 p.m. He has a wife in Ratingen, Germany. We'd like to have your help in having the local police there notify her of his death."

In flawless English, the woman asked for details to pass along to Ratingen police. Clasping the phone between his shoulder and ear and reading from a printout of the story he was holding with both hands, Ed gave her the circumstances surrounding the death, along with names and numbers. The woman said she would call back once the wife was contacted.

"*Danke schön,*" Ed said and hung up, looking pleased at the chance to try out a little German.

Ed remembers another case, years ago, when a Japanese student at Pitt committed suicide. His father worked for a Japanese automaker. Less than twenty-four hours after the death, a limousine pulled up in front of the coroner's office and two company executives got out. The exceedingly polite men handled the entire process, including sending Ed a prepaid envelope so the coroner's office could send the autopsy results back to Japan without delay. This impressed Ed, as did the letter bearing gold-leaf engraving that the company sent to thank the coroner's office for its help.

Laws vary regarding shipping bodies. It can require a good deal of bureaucratic disentanglement to get the body back home. In some countries, the embassy will cover shipping costs; others require the family to pay. Some countries will not take corpses, only cremation ashes. Others take embalmed corpses, but require a special air-sealed casket designed to resist in-flight air pressure changes.

One time, an airline called the coroner's office after the seal on a casket popped mid-flight and the smell of the decomposing corpse filled the passenger plane. The plane landed in Pittsburgh and emptied out quickly. They cleaned the plane, top to bottom, even pulling up the carpeting, before calling the coroner's office to ask how to get rid of the smell. Mike Chichwak suggested fumigation, which the airline said it had tried, without success. Mike was stumped.

It's crucial to make sure you have the right body. Mix-ups do happen, particularly in car crashes with multiple victims. A few weeks earlier, for example, Mike and Tiffani Hunt had stood over a hospital bed in McKeesport, looking back and forth between a dead man's face and a driver's license photo.

The accident had occurred on a highway a few miles away. Two men on a motorcycle were fleeing police when they ran into the side of a sedan. One man was thrown 120 feet, the other 211 feet. One man was still alive, for now, and was flown to a larger hospital in the city. The man at this hospital probably had died at the scene, but they brought him here to make sure. Police gave Mike and Tiffani a pair of overalls with the driver's license in them, but in the aftermath of the crash and rescue efforts there was some uncertainty concerning who had been wearing the overalls before paramedics cut them off at the scene. They weren't sure which man had been driving the motorcycle, a distinction that could prove important if the case went to court.

Mike held the driver's license next to the dead man's head. The young man had a dense, close-trimmed beard. His skin and hair were coal against the snowy sheets of the hospital bed, so dark that it was hard to make out the purple-red asphalt burn on his left shoulder. Everyone looked at the photo and then the man. Tiffani thought it *might* be him, but it was tough to say for sure. The guy in the photo had shoulder-length braids, and the guy in bed had short hair. Also, the dead man looked thicker across the face and shoulders than the photo. Of course, he was only twenty-four, and the photo was taken in 1996, four years earlier. He may have just bulked up.

"Kind of hard to tell," Mike said.

Mike pulled the sheet down further, revealing a tattoo that arced across the man's muscular stomach. In dark script letters, it read: GANGSTER FOR LIFE.

"A 'Gangster for Life' tattoo," Mike said. "Hmm."

The tattoo gave him an idea.

"The Duquesne police said they have a warrant out on the one guy," Mike said. "Would they have information about his tattoo in that case?"

If the warrant mentioned the gangster tattoo, Mike reasoned, then they would have a name—they would know that the two motorcyclists' licenses were switched at the scene. Otherwise, they probably had the right guy. A county homicide detective ran down the warrant. It contained no mention of the gangster tattoo, and it turned out they had the right guy after all. That family wouldn't have to come into the coroner's office to identify the body.

Nowadays, visiting the dead has little of the grandeur that it had when the coroner's chapel was in operation. The coroner's office rarely allows families to see bodies in the flesh—they don't want a grieving mother to throw herself on a body, marring evidence. So instead, they show people to the small chamber they call the crying room.

The crying room—sometimes called the smoking room for self-evident reasons—is small and benignly bland, like a waiting room. It contains three stark blue couches, a hanging spider plant and a small television set in one corner. When an ID is needed, the family members view the body on the TV, which is connected via closed circuit to a video camera mounted on the ceiling of the hallway next to the cooler. A deputy coroner wheels the John or Jane Doe out of the cooler, unzips the body bag and positions the corpse's face underneath the video camera. If the dead person's face is damaged, the deputy may show the witness another part of the corpse's body. The TV is black and white, to mute the effect of bloodstains, bruises, or trauma.

In the case today, the body has already been identified, so they will not use the video camera. This identification is just for the family. The Polaroid snapshot partially covered with tape will do.

Seven minutes after entering the crying room, Jimmy comes out looking glum. No miracles for this mother. The meeting yielded two bits of information—the correct date of birth and spelling of the dead man's name. A few moments later, one of the women rushes out of the room. She asks the receptionist for smelling salts. The dead man's mother has passed out. The receptionist asks Jimmy, who hurriedly checks a first-aid kit in the investigative office but finds nothing. The receptionist calls upstairs and a few moments later, a senior deputy comes down, holding a small paper packet between his fingers.

But the door to the crying room opens before he gets there and the mother lurches out, supported on either side by the two black-jacketed men. She is heavy and sobbing and wearing a gray New York Yankees jacket. The men carrying her wave off the smelling salts.

The senior deputy proffers them again. "You sure you don't want any meds?"

One of the men takes the packet this time. The family lurches out the door and onto the street, and it's over. Over for now; the family will likely return if the suspected killer is caught and a coroner's inquest is held.

An air of discontent settles over the investigative office. No matter how many times it happens, you never quite get used to these scenes. Jimmy sits down at his computer and stares at the case story on the screen. To nobody in particular, he mutters: "And that's why we don't like family members coming in here."

Tracy has kept quiet and watched. Now, out the window, she can see the family limping up the street. The mother sits down heavily on a concrete planter on the corner, staring at the ground. A few minutes later, a dark car pulls up. The men help her into the car and the family drives away.

FOUR

NEXT OF KIN

A couple weeks earlier, halfway through a slow evening shift, Ed Strimlan had leaned against the metal filing cabinets in the investigative office and remarked how few people in Pittsburgh were dying lately. Most mornings the corpse cooler had held just one or two fresh bodies, never more than four. The last seven days were particularly slow, just a dozen bodies. "But the average will come back," Ed said to the other deputy coroners on the evening shift, Mike Chichwak and Tiffani Hunt. "It always does."

Ed was right. As June began and temperatures rose into the eighties, people began dying in scads. Dying unnaturally. A man died in the back of a police wagon. A thirty-five-year-old woman shotgunned herself in the stomach. A forty-eight-year-old man on a cocaine binge blew a blood vessel in his head. A thirty-nine-year-old man hung himself. A twenty-six-year-old man flew from California to Pittsburgh to collect a drug debt and got shot in the chest. A fifty-year-old man wearing headphones and walking along a railroad track didn't hear a train coming.

A few days after Ed's prediction, a pathologist and a homicide detective had a similar conversation in the investigative office. "We *were* doing one or two autopsies a day," the pathologist said. "Now we're doing five or six."

The detective nodded his head. "That's how it goes."

After several busy days, the flood of bodies has slowed down again, at least for tonight, the Wednesday-evening shift. On slow nights, people usually watch TV—*Who Wants to Be a Millionaire?* is a favorite this summer. Interns bring books—often one by Cyril Wecht or Patricia Cornwell—as if they will be accused of slacking if they're reading a book devoid of forensics. (Tracy McAninch breaks this rule, although her reading choices seem significant too; she's reading *Brave New World*.) Some nights people keep to themselves; other times they swap stories or office gossip. The smokers wait until the bosses leave, then light up, sending blossoming clouds to the ceiling of the investigative office. Michael DeRosa plays computer games, massacring aliens, his blueberry eyes glaring at the screen. Ed Strimlan checks stocks online.

Most deputy coroners enjoy the occasional leisurely stretch. They view slow hitches as compensation for the bad stuff—the grief-stricken families, the bad smells, the politics, gore, the odd looks when they stop into Burger King in their coroner's uniforms. In exchange for all that, they get the occasional shift where nobody dies by homicide, suicide, or accident.

But slow shifts make some deputy coroners restless. One midnight-turn deputy periodically bounces up to wipe down all the surfaces of the investigative office with a piney antiseptic spray, or he heads down to the garage to scrub and polish the wagons until they shine. Mike Chichwak is another energetic one. If there are no cases to follow up, he will occupy himself with paperwork or filing or running mail across the street. Even with rush hour approaching, he'd rather be on the road than in the office, so today, with nothing going on, he decides to take some bodies to the crematorium.

Before leaving, Mike tells Ed Strimlan that some family members may be stopping by tonight: the brother of the overdose victim from Beltzhoover, the hairdresser. The brother is the police officer up in Michigan, the one Mike tracked down two nights ago, and he's in town to take care of his brother's effects. He's a cop, so he will get special treatment, a courtesy from one law-enforcement branch to another. Ed understands this unspoken rule. His father was a police officer, too.

Ed and Mike have worked together for so long that they rarely have to confer about such things. They started at the coroner's office about a decade ago and have spent seven years together on the evening shift, a longer partnership than any other pair of deputy coroners. So long that, while working a case, they intuitively know who will interview the survivors and who will rifle the medicine cabinet. Who will grab the legs and who the arms.

With his head of glossy white hair, Ed Strimlan looks about the same age as Mike, who is fifty, but he's actually a decade younger. Ed is large-framed, and his big belly stretches his white deputy shirt so it is continually breaking free from his belt. The gold name tag glinting on the uniform shirt pocket reads DR. EDWARD STRIMLAN.

In 1986, Ed graduated from the American University of the Caribbean School of Medicine on the island of Montserrat. But he failed the licensing examinations for foreign medical graduates, and he never practiced medicine. In 1990, he became a deputy coroner, the eyes and ears of the office's forensic pathologists. Ed likes to say that his MD stands for manic-depressive, but it's clear that he is proud of his medical knowledge. It riles him, for instance, when the homicide commander demands that the deputy coroners bring along one of the coroner's office pathologists to inspect a body at the scene, as if Ed hasn't investigated thousands of deaths over the years, including many dozens of homicides. As if Ed is just a garbageman, there to haul away the remains.

None of the other deputy coroners went to medical school. They have varied backgrounds: a truck driver, a jail guard, an assistant of a local politician. Mike was a paramedic, and Tiffani a high school student who worked at the coroner's office during her summers. Almost all of them have side jobs to supplement their modest paychecks. (Deputy coroners belong to a union, and new hires start at $25,000 a year; they get a raise of $3,500 when they pass the state licensing exam.) One is a gas-station cashier, another a funeral-home embalmer. There is a landscaper, a janitor, and a high school shop teacher. Tiffani is working toward a college degree, Mike helps out at his girlfriend's funeral home and Ed works at a retail farm.

Mike and Ed also run a modest business selling T-shirts, sweatshirts and baseball caps out of the coroner's office. Some articles bear the Allegheny

County Coroner's Office logo; others are less official. One T-shirt shows the white chalk outline of a dead body sprawled over the word CORONER. Another shows a picture of the Grim Reaper, surrounded by the words: CORONER—WHEN YOUR DAY ENDS—OUR DAY BEGINS! The Los Angeles County Coroner's Office actually operates an entire gift shop called Skeletons in the Closet that is full of similar items, but Mike and Ed simply keep the clothes in their lockers at work. They've rejected a few suggestions as being in poor taste, such as a T-shirt that would read: CORONER'S OFFICE—WE WANT YOUR BODY. They believe "Reaper Wear," as they call the business, should be taken in the spirit of good fun. Firefighters and cops love the shirts. Mike is always trying to drum up business, particularly when a new crop of interns arrives. Earlier this week, he showed Tracy and Carey the gear. No commitments yet, but Carey looked interested.

Some deputies seem content at the coroner's office. They get respect from the law enforcement community, and to some, being a small part of the local power structure is satisfying, even though the money is meager. They sometimes work high-profile deaths, the cases people around town are talking about, and even make the paper or TV once in a while. Many are devoted to Cyril Wecht; simply being within his sphere of influence seems to be enough for them.

Others want to move on someday. Tiffani wants to be a physician's assistant, and others are working toward becoming private investigators or following in the footsteps of former deputy coroners who now work for the FBI.

The official requirements for the job are not remarkable: deputy coroners must be able to lift one hundred pounds, have a minimum of two years of higher education, understand some medical terminology, and be able to type thirty-five words a minute. Many get the job through connections, a friend or relative who is a police detective or local officeholder.

The training of death investigators, or lack thereof, has been condemned for decades. Criminals are getting away with murder, critics say, because deputy coroners don't know an exit wound from an entrance wound. Many attribute the lack of training to a general lack of political interest in death investigation. In other words, dead people don't vote.

According to a 1997 report in the *American Journal of Forensic Medicine and Pathology*, most lay death investigators come from three backgrounds: law enforcement, the funeral industry or medicine. The cops know investigation, the report suggests, but lack medical knowledge and are "rough" on survivors. The morticians know anatomy and are good with grieving families but lack investigative skills. The paramedics and nurses know medicine, of course, but may be uncomfortable with investigation and dead bodies. The report named Pennsylvania as one of seven states that require training for death investigators.

To fulfill that requirement, each deputy coroner in Pittsburgh undergoes an initial forty-six-hour death investigation training course in the state capital. In addition, they sit in on a daylong seminar once a year. This year, coroner's school was held at the Allegheny County Coroner's Office in mid-May. Half of the coroner's staff and deputy coroners from small nearby counties gathered in the coroner's office courtroom to listen to seven speakers. (The rest of the deputies will undergo coroner's school in the fall.) At the seminar, a death-scene photographer clicked through a slide show of bloodied torsos, walls spattered with blood, and prisoners hanging from makeshift nooses. The emphasis, the photographer said, is on clarity and comprehensiveness. "We're not trying to produce J.C. Penney catalog photos here," the photographer said. "We're trying to document a scene, and it's not always pretty."

An insect expert discussed forensic entomology, the study of insects that feed and hatch eggs on corpses. It's the most precise way to estimate time of death, he said. Bluebottle flies, for example, can smell a corpse from a mile away. Within minutes of death, these flies will have lit on a body and laid eggs. (Flies appear so quickly, in fact, that scientists in past centuries believed that dead flesh spontaneously spawned its own flies.) Entomologists evaluate the age and type of the developing larvae and pupae offspring, then work backward in time to pinpoint the time of death. As time goes on, various types of beetles, spiders, mites, and millipedes arrive in predictable waves, giving entomologists more markers with which to judge the time of death.

But this method is more difficult than it sounds. Although the information may be used to extract a confession or track down leads, a court will not accept entomological evidence unless it is accurate, which makes for a lot of work at the death scene. Dead flies and maggots and pupae and empty pupa cases must be collected and put in containers filled with a solution of 80 percent alcohol. Live specimens should be collected and given morsels of meat to feed on until they can be examined. Different species must be put in separate containers so they don't eat each other. The temperature of maggot masses must be recorded, along with the ambient temperature around the body and the general weather and environmental circumstances. Soil near the body should be collected. All of these factors can affect an entomologist's findings. Perhaps as a result, the coroner's office rarely bothers with entomological evidence. By the end of the entomologist's presentation, which was littered with words like "larval instar" and "accumulated degree-hours," the deputy coroners were shifting in their seats.

Ed wasn't at coroner's school that day, but he would have found the speech interesting. That's the way his mind works—it soaks up data on topics from horticulture to heart disease. Mike might have enjoyed the entomology lesson, too. Ed and Mike share other similarities. Both of them are nosy—they enjoy nothing more than rooting around someone's house for clues to the victim's lifestyle or death. Both have medical backgrounds, Ed with his medical degree and Mike with his years of ambulance driving. Both are sizable men who can handle their end of a 300-pounder. Neither of them ever gets visibly grossed out, and neither gets stressed out. They are both temperamentally suited to the unpredictability of this job.

But Ed and Mike do have their differences. Mike always climbs into the driver's seat of the wagon because he knows Ed would rather look out the window. Mike likes to hang around the scene for a couple minutes after they're done to shoot the breeze with the cops—it's only polite, he figures, since the cops usually have been hanging around for an hour or two before the deputy coroners show up. Around the office, Ed is a jokester—hands jammed in his pockets like Jay Leno, his one-liners cracking everybody up. Mike started at the coroner's office a few months earlier than Ed but for some bureaucratic reason makes twelve cents less per paycheck, a disparity he often points out on payday. Mike also gives Ed a hard time about never wanting to grab a beer after the shift is over. Ed feels bad about it but just shrugs. He works two jobs and needs to spend any extra time with his kids and wife. Mike, who is divorced with older kids, doesn't have that concern.

Ed and Mike will continue to run the T-shirt business, but their partnership as deputy coroners is coming to an end. At the end of June, Ed is switching to the day shift. His two children are growing up—young Eddie is seven now, a big-framed kid like his father and a slugger on his baseball team, but Ed misses a lot of games working two jobs. During the day, he works at Trax Farm, a 750-acre cropland and market just beyond the edge of the southern suburbs. Like his father and grandfather before him, Ed has worked at the farm on and off since he was twelve. Twenty-eight years. Every summer, Ed brings fresh sweet corn from the farm into the coroner's office. Mike has the cooking down—wrap a cob in a damp towel and microwave for eighty seconds.

One day last month, hosing down flats of seedlings in one of the farm's ten greenhouses, Ed did some mental calculations. Five years earlier he'd borrowed money in order to consolidate his debts, including his medical-school loans. In one month, he'd make the last loan payment. Now Ed figures he can quit his job at Trax and switch to the day shift at the coroner's office to give him more time with his family.

On the down side, Ed knows he likely won't find another partner with Mike's combination of compassion and persistence. These qualities keep Ed, no slacker himself, on his toes. He knows he will miss working with Mike.

After speaking to Ed about the overdose's brother, Mike drags three gurneys down to the basement garage and loads the laden body bags into a wagon. A seventy-six-year-old man who died from colon cancer. A fifty-one-year-old man who died of acute renal failure. A seventy-four-year-old woman who died of a subdural hematoma. No open-casket funerals await these bodies.

No caskets at all. These bodies are wards of the state and are about to be disposed of as simply and cheaply as possible. The back of the wagon is wide enough to fit only two body bags laid side by side, but Mike puts all three in, shoving the woman on top of the two men, her body bag about half the weight of the men's. He muscles her inside with no particular care.

The old lady gets no special treatment today, but her autopsy four weeks ago was a painstaking one. She is a tiny, withered black woman with sagging skin. When she died, the hospital called the coroner's office because they could find no next of kin. The doctors there had diagnosed her as having a subdural hematoma, a blood clot that presses against the brain.

Dr. Bennet Omalu was in charge of autopsies that day, supervised by Dr. Shaun Ladham. A tech was preparing to slice open the scalp when into the autopsy room strode Dr. Cyril Wecht, head of the coroner's office. When Wecht isn't elsewhere in the country—scrutinizing autopsy records and crime-scene photos for a private client or discussing the latest famous cases, such as JFK Jr. or JonBenet, with Geraldo Rivera—he begins his day by bustling through the autopsy room to get a bulletin on the day's deaths. Despite their regularity, Wecht's morning appearances are dramatic and seem to invigorate the autopsy staff like a slug of extra-strong coffee. He is a brisk blur of energy, sharp eyes darting, his bald, tan head bobbing, the loose ends of his tie flapping around his expensive-looking gray suit, as if he's simply too rushed to finish his dressing.

It's hard to predict which case will interest him from one morning to the next. Local newspaper columnists ridicule his reputed lust for publicity and his frequent press conferences about high-profile cases. But Wecht will often warn his subordinates to be alert for inconsistencies in seemingly routine cases.

On this day, Wecht bypassed another case—an old man who had shot himself in the mouth. Ed and Mike had picked him up the night before. Wecht glanced at the old man, hurriedly saying, "Good, good," and moved away. But he stopped when the pathologists mentioned that the little old lady on the other table had lived in a personal care home. Wecht set down his briefcase and delivered a short harangue about the lack of regulations surrounding the institutions.

"It's almost like anybody can take in some people and call themselves a personal care home," Wecht told the pathologists.

Wecht's message was clear—this seemingly routine death could have been caused by neglect, careless policies, or even homicide. The woman may have fallen and cracked her head due to neglect or some careless action by the personal care home staff. The previous autumn, for instance, a seventy-six-year-old woman had fallen down a flight of stairs at a personal care home. She received no medical treatment for her injuries for six days, until her daughter noticed bruises on her mother's torso. She died a few weeks later and was buried because the coroner's office was unaware of the details surrounding her death. Later, the coroner's office examined the medical record and held an open inquest into the case. Wecht ruled that no criminal charges were warranted, but said the nursing home mishandled her treatment and the reporting of the death.

In today's case, Wecht opined, perhaps the nursing home had not carefully screened its personnel, and an aide with homicidal tendencies had abused the old lady. A year before, a mentally retarded man died after an overworked and frustrated personal care home aide admitted that he had grabbed the retarded man, accidentally knocking him down. In that case, Wecht did recommend the district attorney file homicide charges.

And this is why Wecht and others support the coroner system. Wecht understands the arguments of those who say Pennsylvania should adopt a medical-examiner system. He is aware of the faults of the coroner system—primarily, the fact that many lack adequate training. After all, he helped lead the fight in the early 1960s to oust his coroner's office predecessor, arguing that a cabinetmaker with no medical training should not run a crucial medicolegal government facility.

But Wecht supports the coroner system because it offers two crucial advantages: independence and legal authority. As an elected, not appointed, office, a coroner's office has the power to make decisions based on science and law, not pressure from other agencies or politicians. This is a significant distinction, Wecht argues, one that allows him to regularly criticize or even conduct open inquests into controversial deaths, such as those involving police or major airlines or nursing homes. Wecht maintains that friends of his, high-profile medical examiners in Los Angeles and New York City, were forced out of office when local politicians didn't like their findings. In Pittsburgh, the coroner's office needs nobody's blessing when it decides to start holding hearings and issuing subpoenas.

It is the job of the coroner's office to rule out wrongdoing in deaths like the old lady at the nursing home. Of course, such a finding could lead to headlines, state hearings—or even a chapter in one of Wecht's popular books about offbeat cases he's worked. Throughout his career, Wecht has always sought that elusive detail, that snippet of evidence someone else would miss, the clue that would have gone unnoticed before 1965, when Wecht became the county's chief forensic pathologist.

But the case of the little old lady turned out to be no headline grabber. When Wecht left the room, the pathologists made sure of that, peeling back the scalp even further than usual to hunt for skull fractures or bruises in the underside of the scalp. When they popped the skull, a dark raspberry-jelly mass of blood covered the right side of the brain. The pathologists painstakingly scraped and tweezed the tough skin of the dura mater off the inside of the skull and wiped down the bone surface with a paper towel, but they found no fracture that would indicate the bleeding was caused by trauma to the skull. No foul play.

And, as it turned out, the woman had not been living at the personal care home at the time of her death. The home had closed down, deputy coroners discovered, and a friend had taken the woman in. Deputy coroners quizzed the friend and made all the routine calls but found no next of kin. The woman had no family at all, the friend said, and subsisted on a monthly Social Security check of $539. Her body lay on a gurney in the cooler for almost four weeks, until this slow afternoon when Mike decided to take her and the other two bodies to the crematorium.

Now her body is in the back of the coroner's wagon, rumbling toward its final destination. The other two corpses died about a month ago also. The seventy-six-year-old man's only relative was a retarded son with no income. The fifty-one-year-old man lived in a homeless shelter and had no family. One reason deputy coroners work so hard to find next of kin is because the county doesn't want to be responsible for these bodies.

If the deceased is a Catholic, the St. Vincent De Paul Society may pay for a burial, as it has for almost a hundred and fifty years. Other Christian and Jewish organizations sometimes perform a similar function. The federal government buries indigent veterans. In the past, the owner of a local Chinese restaurant buried Chinese people who died in Pittsburgh without family or money. Sometimes a family member or a friend will contact the coroner's office after a week or two and say they have scraped together enough money for a simple funeral service. Sometimes they call too late. Mike remembers one woman who came into the office and inquired about a relative she had tracked down to Pittsburgh. It turned out he had died homeless and the county had paid for his cremation and burial . . . three years earlier.

In 1983, a custodian found the body of a teenage boy in the chimney of an elementary school on Mount Washington. Hot air from a heating duct had dehydrated the body, helping to preserve it. Police believed the body belonged to a sixteen-year-old who had disappeared more than four years earlier. They speculated that the boy, who was seen walking near the school after a New Year's Eve party, had crawled or fallen into the chimney, perhaps to get warm. Although the clothing, size, and age of the body resembled those of the missing boy, the family refused to believe that the body was his. So the body lay in the morgue freezer, a state of limbo that lasted for two and a half years, until a local priest read about the situation and offered the boy his own burial plot. In 1986, more than seven years after the missing boy's death, the priest and seven teenagers from his parish carried the casket and flowers to the grave site and recited the rosary before the burial.

But most unclaimed bodies become the county's responsibility, a long-standing practice. A few years ago, someone found an old wooden box in the building's basement that turned out to be a bound logbook. Inside were pages and pages of yellowing photos from the 1940s and '50s—head shots of corpses that were cremated at the county's expense. No names or details about the deaths were recorded, just the date and the black and white photos, heads thrown back, covered with sheets up to their necks, eyes open or shut.

No family or friends had claimed the bodies Mike loaded into the wagon, so students at a local mortuary school washed and embalmed them for free. Now, the county will pay $120 apiece for a simple cremation. Their ashes will be put in a concrete vault that will hold the remains of up to three hundred people. Sometimes the funeral home will wait for a year or so before burying all these ashes in a mass grave. In Allegheny County, between fifty and seventy bodies a year meet this fate.

Mike drives to a small river town about eight miles up the Allegheny and parks behind a white house that had been converted to a funeral home. A thin, middle-aged woman wearing shorts and a T-shirt comes down the back stairs. She's carrying a baby on her hip. Mike can't resist the baby. "Oh, look at those pretty blue eyes," Mike says, his Pittsburgh rasp softening to a quasi-coo.

"Oh, if you only knew," the woman says.

They laugh and Mike clucks at the baby some more. "Big blue eyes," he says.

The woman points to the wagon. "Are any of them leaking?" she asks. This can be a problem with bodies that have lain in a cooler for a month.

Mike doesn't think so. He unloads the bodies one at a time, rolling the gurneys into the funeral home's back room, then yanking the body bags onto funeral-home gurneys. A blue metal box the size of a pickup truck dominates the small room that otherwise looks like the waiting area of a suburban dentist's office. The box has buttons and lights and a digital temperature monitor. Its door has a small window. Inside the gas-fired chamber is a concrete floor with a body-sized indentation.

The first American cremation took place thirty miles southwest of Pittsburgh, when the corpse of an Austrian baron was burned in 1876. At the time, modernists were promoting cremation as a more sanitary way to dispose of the dead, noting that most ancient cultures burned corpses on open-air pyres until the Christian custom of ground burial swept the western world. Newspapers across the country ran front-page stories attacking or ridiculing the cremation in Washington, Pennsylvania, but cremation supporters had the last laugh. Now, a century and a quarter later, one-fourth of all people in the United States choose to be cremated. Or, as in the case of the three corpses Mike has brought to the funeral home, cremation is chosen for them.

One by one, the corpses will be pushed into the chamber, body bags and all, and burned at 1,800 degrees Fahrenheit. The burning will take two and a half hours or so, probably less for the small woman. Afterward, the ashes will lie in a long pile that approximates the size and shape of a human body, like the ash of a cigarette that was lit and left to burn out in an ashtray. The ashes are actually bone fragments, which the crematory workers sweep into a pan with a metal-handled broom. Cremated remains—cremains—going to a funeral are usually poured into an urn. These bodies will be placed in heavy-grade plastic bags, put in cardboard boxes smaller than shoeboxes, wrapped in brown paper and stacked on top of the pile of identical boxes along the wall. When there are enough boxes to fill an entire vault, the funeral home will bury them together.

The baby watches silently as Mike unloads the bodies. "Such a good baby," Mike says to the woman. "They should all stay that way."

"Yeah, I know," the funeral home woman says.

Back at the office, the phone rings at 5:00 p.m., and Mike picks up. The brother of the overdose victim. He and some other family members are at his brother's apartment on the other side of the river, and he needs directions to the coroner's office. Mike explains how to get down the hill and across the river to Downtown.

After hanging up, Mike heads back to the cooler. He pulls the stretcher out into the hallway and unzips the body bag to expose the head and torso of the overdose. The dead man wears a graying goatee, and his cheeks are whiskery too, like he hasn't shaved in a few days. Often a corpse will develop five-o'clock shadow after a day, but not, as legend has it, because the whiskers keep growing, but because the skin shrinks around the hair follicles. Sometimes, the tiny muscles attached to the follicles stiffen with rigor, pushing out the stubble.

Mike ducks into the empty autopsy room and grabs a towel and sheet. He spreads the sheet over the dead man's body and pulls it up under his chin to hide the autopsy cuts on the chest and stomach. He tucks the towel over the top of the overdose's head to hide the scalp cuts. Mike regards his handiwork, cocking his head slightly. He reaches out and smoothes down a wayward lock of the dead man's blond hair.

When his father died three weeks ago, Mike took nine days off. On his first day back, Mike pulled his truck into the morgue's inadequate parking area almost half an hour early, as usual. Another deputy coroner from the day shift met Mike at the garage door. He told Mike about a pending case, a homicide from another county, a 300-pounder who'd attacked his neighbor a month ago, first with a car antenna, then with a knife. The neighbor had smacked him in the head with a brick, and the man was flown to UPMC-Presbyterian Hospital in Pittsburgh, where he finally died today. And just like that, Mike was back. Like nothing had changed. "OK," Mike said. "Good enough."

A few minutes later, Dr. Leon Rozin came through the office and stopped when he saw Mike. In a murmur thickened by his Ukrainian accent, the office's chief forensic pathologist offered condolences, then asked how old Mike's father was when he died. Seventy-six, Mike said. Rozin asked more questions, and Mike told the story of his father's illness, the angioplasty and stents, the shortness of breath three weeks later, the return to the hospital, the long recovery.

A long white doctor's coat draped over his short frame, Rozin leaned absorbedly against a metal file cabinet. He wanted to know what medication Mike's father was on, and the timing of everything. Ed Strimlan was in by that time, sitting at his desk, listening again to the details he'd heard when he went to the viewing at Elachko Funeral Home. Mike's voice was strong and normal, and he leaned against the filing cabinet too and told the story as if it was just another case—a body Rozin would be cutting open the next day and wanted to know a little more about and that was why he had stopped into the investigative office for a briefing.

His father's cardiac enzymes were elevated, Mike said, which pointed to heart damage. Given the recent angioplasty, the doctors suspected blood had clotted around one of the stents inserted to hold open his narrowing arteries. But when they inserted a catheter into the arteries, the vessels were open. Whatever the cause, the doctors figured he had a slight myocardial infarction— heart tissue damaged from lack of blood.

Anyway, he gradually got better and moved to Braddock Hospital. Then, nine days earlier, Mike had received the call while he was in the flower shop at Elachko. When he got to the hospital, they told him that his father had died. The nurse said he'd been in good spirits earlier that morning, reading the paper, talking to his roommate, kidding his caretakers. Then they found him in the bathroom, slumped against the wall. He said he felt funny. No pain, no shortness of breath, just odd.

"So they put him in a wheelchair, took him to his room, took him into bed," Mike told Rozin. "And he arrested."

Rozin nodded. "That's too bad."

"Yeah, it is," Mike said.

How did the doctors sign out the death certificate, Rozin wanted to know. Probable myocardial infarction leading to heart failure, Mike said. In the manner of someone who solves death for a living, Rozin asked if Mike had requested an autopsy. The procedure could help determine exactly how the heart was damaged and why he died when he did.

No, Mike said. He knew from experience that the heart was a mysterious muscle that could give out or revive in any number of ways. The exact cause of death was unknown, but Mike knew well that an autopsy might not provide precise answers either. Mike had seen plenty of families over the years who demanded autopsies, demanded the cold comfort of scientific conclusions, when it was clear that the body had simply given way to time. And then there were others who balked at postmortems, who didn't want to know, who wanted their relatives buried intact.

Mike felt like this: his father was dead. It just didn't seem important to know exactly what killed him.

Mike didn't tell Rozin how he felt on the trip to the hospital, and the aftermath. He left out how he'd cried, how he couldn't accept his father's death, how he'd damned the timing, that it had happened just when he seemed to be getting better. Mike didn't say how this outpouring of anguish and disbelief had caught him by surprise. Even as the emotion hit, part of him had been astonished that he was reacting just like everybody else, all those people he'd notified about deaths. All those years in the coroner's office and the funeral home and the ambulance, and very few cases really affected Mike anymore, despite his compassion for the survivors. He could pick up a kid who just shot himself or a grandmother who died of neglect and still go home and sleep solidly that night. So it surprised him that, after all these years of death work, he hadn't been ready when it was his turn.

The viewing at Elachko had been strange, too. His father was laid out in the casket, and people were stopping by—friends, family, coworkers from the coroner's office, Ed Strimlan of course. Mike kept getting caught up in talking to people, and he kept reminding himself that it was not just another Elachko client lying there, but his father.

Just as Mike finishes preparing the dead man for the arrival of his brother, an administrator comes through the hall on his way home. "Who's this?" the administrator asks.

"This is the overdose from Monday night," Mike says.

"Poor guy," the administrator says cheerily.

A few minutes later, the buzzer sounds at the front door of the coroner's office, and Mike goes into the entrance hall to greet the four men who come in. All four are ruddy-faced and well-built, just like the dead man. They look like brothers or cousins.

One man wearing a gray T-shirt and a cellular phone clipped to his jeans belt introduces himself as the dead man's brother. Mike asks if his directions were OK, and the men say yes and marvel at the city's hills—so different from Michigan. They talk easily for a few moments, and then Mike says: "I'm sorry we had to meet under these circumstances."

The brother asks Mike when the toxicology results will be available. Twelve weeks, Mike says. The lab is a little backed up. The brother nods. He's not happy with it, but he understands governmental delay. He's a cop.

The brother says they cleaned out the apartment and made arrangements with a funeral director. "This is the last thing we have to do," he says.

The four men trail Mike single-file through the investigative office. Ed and Tiffani and two new interns nod solemnly at them. Mike has already decided he will break protocol and allow the brother to say goodbye in person. No fuzzy Polaroid or crying-room TV screen this time. A courtesy. The brother's a cop.

The gurney stands in the hallway where Mike left it, draped in white. Mike stands aside to let the men pass. The brother approaches first. He doesn't look until he's standing right over the stretcher. Then he looks down. His brother's face is haloed in white cloth, the towel and the sheet. Swaddled, sort of. Like a sleeping baby. But the face itself is red and bristly and ruined.

The brother stares down for a long moment, his eyes filling. Almost unintelligibly, he whispers, "OK," and walks away.

FIVE

THE COURTROOM

All week, ever since the homicide on Monday night, Tiffani has run into people on the street who said they saw her at the crime scene. They were among the restless crowd in the Addison Terrace projects, and they saw her working, wearing the badge. Tiffani knew this would happen. She knows too many people on the Hill to have escaped unrecognized.

On Tuesday night, homicide detectives in the case came to the coroner's office to get an arrest warrant. They had a suspect's name—Ernest Harris, a.k.a. "Pickles," age thirty-one—but they hadn't caught him.

Pickles! Tiffani knew Pickles. A friendly, outgoing guy, but the thing about Pickles was, you never knew what he was going to do. You always heard about him carrying a gun, being involved in shootings. Now this.

The cops wanted Pickles, but they didn't know where to find him. All week they looked, until tonight, Saturday, when the phone rings, and it's the police, saying they have Pickles and they're bringing him over for his arraignment. Tiffani just happens to be working that shift when the call comes in.

Earlier that afternoon, someone called the police and gave them the tip-off: Pickles was holed up in a third-floor apartment on Bentley Drive, right down the street from the homicide, in the same project. The tipster didn't give a name, but the cops went there anyway and surrounded the place. Not eager to break in and arrest him by force, the police first tried calling the apartment. It worked. They got Pickles on the line and convinced him to give himself up.

Now they're on their way over to the coroner's office, the detectives and Pickles. Mike DeRosa is working too, but Tiffani knows DeRosa hates doing arraignments for some reason. He's done only one in five years at the office. So she agrees to do it. It's her job, whether or not she knows the guy. So Tiffani heads up to the third-floor courtroom.

The coroner's office courtroom is about twice as big as an average high school classroom, and like the rest of the coroner's office, it is built in generous, turn-of-the-century fashion: thick brass doorknobs and hinges and a long judge's dais made of dark, heavy wood. Two tables face the dais. During inquests, the defendant and his lawyer sit at one table and the prosecutor sits, often alone, at the other.

This courtroom is where the legal phase of homicide cases begins. Arraignments and inquests take place here—sometimes one a week, sometimes four or five. During inquests, an attorney who works for the coroner's office acts like a magistrate judge does in other kinds of criminal cases. He hears evidence and decides whether the case is strong enough to be tried at the courthouse a block up Ross Street. If not, the accused killer will go free. Either way, some spectators usually leave the coroner's office in torment.

Before inquests begin, two strapping deputy sheriffs search the spectators, sweeping handheld metal detectors up and down each person. They confiscate anything that could be a weapon, even removing a sewing needle from one woman's purse before an inquest last month. They have found razors, knives and guns. (The previous fall, a key prosecution witness came to court carrying a licensed handgun. He refused to go to the witness seat and testify against two accused killers without his weapon. He was ordered off the coroner's office premises, a blow to the prosecution's case.) After spectators mount the two flights of stairs, deputy coroners usher them to their seats, trying to find room for everybody. In some inquests, spectators pack every row of wooden seats all the way to the rear of the courtroom, where listeners must crane their necks to hear over the rattle of the air conditioner in the window. Like guests at a wedding ceremony, the victim's family tends to choose seats behind the prosecutor and the defendant's family behind the defense table. Victims' relatives sometimes carry framed photographs of the deceased, propping them on their laps as if to remind the officials that a real person died.

The inquest proceedings often take place a week or two after the killing, when grief and anger still run hot. Often the onlookers are split; half are related to the deceased and half to the defendant. Squabbles can break out between factions. It's up to the coroner's office employees to keep things calm, because a defense attorney could argue in trial that an unruly atmosphere at an inquest worked against the defendant.

Testimony can be agonizing for survivors. In an inquest last month, an emergency operator reluctantly repeated the exact words she had heard in a 911 call from a man accused of shooting his girlfriend. "He said, 'My fucking girlfriend just shot herself in the fucking neck. Oh shit, she's still breathing.'" A quiver of horror went through the dead woman's family. During another inquest, the dead woman's family could not repress shrieks of anger when the muscular man accused of killing her shuffled into the courtroom, legs bound by ankle cuffs and tattooed tears on his face to mark time already spent behind bars. One woman sprang up and pointed at the accused man, and the inquest hearing officer thundered a warning at her. Later, when a witness repeated the suspect's claim that the shooting was accidental, several crowd members rose in fury. "If there are going to be any more outbursts during this proceeding, I'm going to clear the room in its entirety, which means everybody will leave," the magistrate said. He pointed at a woman who had just yelled. "Ma'am, I'm going to ask you to leave right now." Flanked by two deputies, the distraught woman left.

Coroner's officials may have been edgier than usual that day due to a particularly disorderly inquest a few months earlier. On that day, the courtroom was crowded with friends and family of both the victim and accused. Frustrated with a delay in the proceedings, a spectator began clamoring. Then, when a prosecution witness failed to show, the hearing was postponed, and some in the crowd bickered and chased after each other as they were leaving.

One man approached the sister of one of the accused men and said: "If I can't get your brother, I'm going to get you." Then he pointed a finger at her and pretended to fire a gun. On her way home from the coroner's office, she later told police, the same man pulled up behind her and fired eight shots at her car, hitting it once. She was unharmed.

Bystanders who witness homicides are often afraid to testify for fear of reprisal, a perpetual worry for the prosecution. Even when a witness is placed in the protection program run by the district attorney's office, they sometimes disappear the day of the coroner's inquest. Four months earlier, an accused murderer was released from jail after being hauled to the coroner's office for an inquest four times. In one hearing, the coroner's hearing officer ruled the evidence wasn't strong enough to send the case to trial. The district attorney did more work, refiled charges against the suspect, and brought him in again. But that time, and twice more, a witness failed to show. The district attorney said he would refile the charge again as soon as the witness was located.

Some inquests are big news. Reporters from four television stations and two or three newspapers watch the proceedings from their seats in the rarely used jury box; swarming photographers take turns aiming their lenses at the defendant through the glass pane of the courtroom door. Afterward, the steps outside the coroner's office or the hall outside the courtroom becomes an impromptu backdrop for interviews. Newspeople shout questions as the defendant is ushered away or gather in circles around family members or lawyers, who blink in the blaze of camera lights. For reporters frustrated by the meagerness of details released by police, inquests are a rich source of information about murders. And because the killings usually have happened only days earlier, inquests provide raw, camera-ready emotions. After conducting family interviews during a break in the May inquest into the shooting of a twenty-two-year-old suburban woman, one television reporter asked another: "Did you make anyone cry?"

Another high-profile inquest that month had all the elements of a good news story—youthful tragedy, unexpected death, mystery, an enemy. A young tow-truck driver had died earlier in the month on an interstate highway just outside of Pittsburgh. He'd just loaded a car onto his truck and was standing beside a patrol car, talking to police, when another car struck him, tossing him forty feet. The driver sped away and police could not catch him, but a tip about a damaged car in a mall parking lot the next day led state troopers to the defendant. This inquest attracted several reporters and photographers and led to prominent stories.

Other inquests barely rate a mention in the news. During the inquest into the death of the fifty-nine-year-old flyweight stab victim autopsied by Bennet Omalu in May, the courtroom was positively drowsy. Ten minutes before the proceedings began, one bored television cameraman wearing tennis shoes and shorts loafed in the hallway. The defense attorney was nowhere to be seen, so the assistant district attorney joked around with a deputy coroner and the morgue janitor. The only people with a personal stake in the proceeding were four women. But even these women did not seem overly emotional as they murmured about shopping.

The case—just another killing in a neighborhood known for violence—lacked the intrigue that makes for headlines. On the other hand, the tow-truck driver and the man who ran into him were both young and white and the death was so unpredictable. Newspaper editors and television news producers would say that the abruptness and unforeseen nature of the accident, along with the victim's youth and the outcry in his neighborhood, dictated the heavy coverage of that inquest. Many black Pittsburghers would say that the race of the victim played a part. If reporters had dug deeper into the second case, they could have found newsworthy elements in the victim's size (110 pounds) and age and the brutality of the killing.

But they did not. Two cameramen and one television reporter showed for the proceeding. Neither of the city's two major newspapers ran stories about it the next day.

The courtroom is also where the roles of the police and the coroner's office collide. Those roles often don't conflict—police and the district attorney's office have gathered evidence against an accused killer and it's solid enough for the coroner's office to hold the case for court. However, a good forensic pathologist or deputy coroner has to learn to work alongside police without catering to them or molding evidence to suit the prosecutor's case. They haven't always been so independent and honest; in Texas and West Virginia, for example, forensic experts allegedly have lied about DNA and autopsies, giving false testimony that led to convictions.

Timothy Uhrich, the hearing officer in coroner's inquests, also has to make sure he doesn't automatically side with the district attorney. A year before, for instance, police arrested a man named Thomas Craighead after a twenty-three-year-old man was found dead on the sidewalk outside an Oakland bar, shot through the heart. In the coroner's inquest, a witness said he saw Craighead shoot toward a group of men outside the bar. A defense attorney argued that the deadly bullet could have been fired by one of the other men in the group, and Uhrich dismissed the case, saying "no causal connection" existed between the witness's testimony and the dead man. Police were stunned. Two months later, the district attorney refiled charges against Craighead, and brought two more witnesses to testify at the inquest. This time, Uhrich ruled there was enough evidence to hold the case for trial.

Relations between police and the coroner's office grow the most strained when a death involves a police officer. Wecht would say that this is when the political independence of the coroner system is most crucial.

Perhaps the most rancorous police-related death investigation in coroner's office history occurred in 1995, when five white suburban police officers pulled over a black motorist named Jonny Gammage. A fight broke out and the officers wrestled Gammage to the ground, where Gammage lost consciousness and later died. An autopsy found that pressure on his chest and neck was the cause. The case attracted national headlines, and Gammage's parents hired Wecht, who was working as a private forensic pathologist at the time, to conduct a second autopsy. (That year, Wecht was reelected as Allegheny County Coroner after fifteen years away from the job.) Three officers faced charges of involuntary manslaughter, and Wecht criticized the way they restrained Gammage.

"You have five police officers [and] one man who is not posing a threat," Wecht said on the stand during one officer's 1996 trial. "If he runs away, it's not a great tragedy. He had not committed any crime. They didn't like the way he was driving. What was the urgency, what was the necessity for these five police officers to be subduing him to the extent that they were?"

Later that same day, Wecht suggested that the officer himself should take the stand, which triggered a mistrial, because the judge decided that Wecht's words might prejudice the jury against the officer. After two mistrials and an acquittal, charges were eventually dropped against all three officers.

Wecht relishes a good fight with the powers that be, even when he himself is in power. This seems fitting for a man who launched his public career by saying that the official investigation of a presidential assassination was untrustworthy, and followed it up with one anti-establishment finding after another. Sirhan Sirhan did not kill Senator Robert F. Kennedy; a second shooter fired the fatal bullet. Elvis Presley most likely died from the combination of codeine, Valium, and other sedatives in his blood, not from heart problems. As an expert witness, Wecht still suffers for his decision to help Fox television producers analyze an "alien autopsy" for a 1995 special, even though he drew few firm conclusions about the validity of the "extraterrestrial." When he gets on the witness stand, opposing attorneys bring up the show in an effort to discredit him. They also bring up articles he has written for the *National Enquirer* and *Gallery*, a men's magazine, about the JFK assassination. But Wecht seems to regret nothing from his past, not even the alien autopsy show. ("I said it was like no human body I'd ever seen and it requires further study and investigation," Wecht says. "There is nothing to regret.")

Local newspaper columnists and rivals also mock him regularly as a headline-monger, but Wecht insists he is led not by politics but by science. If the evidence points to homicide, he recommends homicide, whether the killer is a career criminal or a cop.

The relationship between the county's various police departments and the coroner's office has been tested recently. Throughout most of the '90s, all police officers in more than a dozen death cases were cleared of criminal charges. Some cases seemed to be obvious self-defense. One city police officer was being dragged by a stolen car when he opened fire, killing the vehicle's driver and two occupants. Other cases, like the death of unarmed Jonny Gammage, were less clear-cut. In recent months, however, Wecht has recommended that the district attorney's office file homicide charges against police officers in three separate cases involving shootings after police chases.

The year before, Wecht helped resurrect a 1995 case against a Pittsburgh Housing Authority police officer, recommending the officer be charged with criminal homicide. A city police officer began chasing a motorist who was going the wrong way on a one-way street. Other police joined the chase, which ended in the Armstrong Tunnels, a few blocks from the coroner's office. There, several police officers opened fire. Officer John Charmo fired thirteen of the fourteen bullets that hit and killed the man. He later claimed that the dead man had spun his car around inside the tunnels and driven at the police officers. After a coroner's inquest, no charges were filed against the officers. But last year, Wecht launched a second investigation into the case, saying that wheel markings on the pavement inside the tunnels contradicted Charmo's claim that he was in danger. "The car did not turn," Wecht said during a press conference.

Around the same time, Wecht recommended that another city police officer, who shot a man after a chase, be charged with homicide. After that case, Wecht tried to reform the way local police handle car chases, recommending that they buy tire-deflation devices to be carried in the trunk of every patrol car and have the police accident-investigation unit help investigate car-chase deaths in conjunction with homicide detectives.

But it happened again anyway. The previous fall, a suburban police officer shot a man after another police chase. The man died a week later, and Wecht recommended that the district attorney file homicide charges against the officer. A couple months ago, a county homicide detective who investigated the case wrote a letter to the local Fraternal Order of Police saying the coroner's inquest was "farcical," "unreasonable," and "obviously biased." He said Wecht misstated another officer's testimony concerning the danger facing police at the shooting scene. Wecht, of course, fired back with his own letter, writing that the officer had "deliberately contaminated" the case. Despite Wecht's recommendation of homicide, the district attorney has not yet filed charges against the police officer.

Wecht knows his stances in these cases, especially the Gammage matter, have created some resentment among police. Police don't like their decisions to be questioned, he says, especially rank-and-file officers. But the chiefs tend to understand Wecht's duties better, he says, and even the lower officers have become resigned to the fact that when someone dies, it's not the police who run the show, but the coroner's office.

Eleven days earlier, it happened once again: another police-related death, though this time it involved no gunplay or car chase. A thirty-one-year-old man went berserk on a street in Uptown, throwing himself against cars. Police officers tried to subdue the man, then sprayed him with pepper spray. They handcuffed him and put him in the back of a police van, where he banged his head against the wall on the way to the hospital. A doctor listened to the arrested man's heart and lungs, which seemed normal. The man refused mental health treatment, and the police officers took him to jail. He continued to bang his head on the van's walls. At the jail, when they opened the doors, the man was lying face-up on the floor, dead.

Police pulled the body out of the van and laid it on a cot in the jail garage, where medics cut off his sweatpants and injected epinephrine to stimulate his heart, with no luck. Mike Chichwak was on duty when the city police homicide commander called the coroner's office at 8:22 p.m. He and another deputy coroner drove the few short blocks to the jail, a big, blocky, red-brick structure on the banks of the Monongahela near the edge of Downtown. Mike noted the dead man's forehead and eyes were bruised and abraded. He took down the police officers' stories—as white cops in the post-Gammage era, they were petrified about their involvement with a dead black man.

The next morning, Dr. Bennet Omalu performed the autopsy. He recorded the abrasions on the head, but when the autopsy techs popped the skull, he found no fractures or hemorrhage. The autopsy proved little except that the man did not die from head trauma, exonerating the police officers from any possible charge that they may have beaten him to death. A couple hours later, almost two dozen people—coroner's staffers, reporters, family members, and homicide detectives—gathered in the coroner's office courtroom for a press conference on the autopsy findings. When Wecht strode into the courtroom, one homicide detective turned quietly to another.

"Let the show begin," he muttered under his breath.

Wecht took his place at a table bristling with microphones, folded his hands in front of his face and began summarizing the case in a low-key tone. The cause of death was undetermined, pending further tests. The dead man had prescriptions for blood-pressure medication and an antidepressant. Mixed with alcohol or drugs, those medications could have proven fatal. Pepper spray has killed people before, Wecht said, but if the dead man had been hypersensitive to the irritant, he probably would have reacted immediately.

As he spoke, Wecht's words grew faster. His eyebrows lifted to emphasize particular points and his head bobbed. He gripped his chair's wooden armrests. Wecht spoke freely about what he knew and what he didn't know, reading unrehearsed snippets straight from a hospital report at one point. *Let the show begin*—this is what the detective had meant. And the reporters loved it, even as they glanced knowingly at each other—vintage Wecht, a press conference where information gushed like water from a fire hydrant, rather than being doled out in the usual calculated doses. Before the reporters' eyes, Wecht transformed from longtime member of the local establishment to the relentlessly curious and outspoken forensic pathologist he is.

Wecht was especially intrigued by the fact that the dead man had been taken to the same hospital earlier in the day, before he went berserk on the street. And in the hospital records, a nurse had listed cocaine as one of the drugs in the dead man's system. In combination with other drugs, cocaine could have killed him. Perhaps cocaine had heightened his sensitivity to pepper spray. Any number of possibilities existed, Wecht said, waving a hand.

"We have to find out from the nurse where she got that information," he said, his face looking tanner than ever in the glow of the TV lights. "I cannot tell you at this time. I do not know. We'll have to learn more about it. But blood was drawn. Well, we'll find out. It's very interesting."

Tonight, when Tiffani reaches the third floor, the coroner's office court-room is silent and empty. The arraignment of Pickles will be a much quieter affair than any inquest or press conference. If the papers or TV stations are tipped off to an arraignment, they may send photographers over to get pictures of the defendant on the "perp walk." But little usually happens during an arraignment—it is simply the formal reading of charges against the defendant—so the proceedings rarely rate a reporter's presence.

Since nobody is going to show up except Pickles and the detectives, Tiffani doesn't even bother to sit behind the judge's dais. It just seems so formal. So instead she gets a sheet of paper that contains the questions she is supposed to ask the defendant—whether he has a lawyer, whether he understands the charges against him—and takes a seat at the prosecutor's table. On weekdays, the coroner's office solicitor, Timothy Uhrich, the same deputy coroner who acts as a magistrate during inquests, handles arraignments. But it's a weekend night, so it's up to the deputy coroners.

When the homicide detectives lead Pickles into the courtroom, the tall, good-looking defendant is in street clothes and handcuffs. He is smiling and joking, which seems sort of weird.

Then he catches sight of Tiffani and shouts out: "Hey! I know you! You went to Schenley High School. You live on the Hill."

Tiffani did go to Schenley, but that's not where Pickles knows her from. He's wrong about that. She is ten years younger than he is, so they never would have run into each other in high school. No, Pickles is just one of the dozens, hundreds of people Tiffani knows casually on the Hill. For one thing, Pickles's brother is the best friend of the father of Tiffani's baby. Also, she used to go with Pickles's cousin. She's even been in his family's house, she's pretty sure.

That's how it is on the Hill. Everybody is connected to each other in a bunch of different ways. Like a spider web. But Tiffani doesn't know how to react when he yells out his greeting—she's arraigning this guy for murder and he acts like they just ran into each other at some club Uptown. So Tiffani just squints at him and doesn't say anything.

It doesn't matter. Pickles starts joking around with the detectives, even talking about the shooting, *joking* about it, the fact that they found a .38-caliber bullet casing at the scene.

I'm a .44-caliber man, he's saying. *I don't know where you're coming from with that .38-caliber stuff.*

Like everybody always said, you never knew what Pickles was going to do.

SIX

DEATH, BE NOT PROUD

Carey Welch holds open the heavy metal door as Tracy McAninch walks into the corpse cooler, shoving an empty gurney ahead of her. They've just returned from the garage, where they helped a deputy coroner sign over a body to a funeral home director. Tracy clanks the empty gurney up against the others, some bearing bodies, some not.

"Watch and make sure nobody reaches out and grabs me," Tracy calls over her shoulder to Carey, only half joking.

It's another Monday evening, and Tracy is beginning to feel more comfortable at the coroner's office. She's had five days off since her first Monday-evening/Tuesday-morning pair of shifts. In the first days, the images of her first shifts stuck with her. Especially the young black guy from the Hill District with the bullet hole in his aorta. Something about him being so young and fit made it worse. As the days passed, however, her memory of the shocking sights and sounds began to dim. Her friends pestered her for details about what she'd witnessed. She told one friend about Ed and Mike's T-shirt business, laughing at the shirt that said WHEN YOUR DAY ENDS—OUR DAY BEGINS! That friend said she was sick, like it wasn't funny, and Tracy wondered if she was changing already, growing desensitized like the others.

But it's hard to be serious at the coroner's office, especially when you're working with Ed Strimlan. Earlier, Tracy rode with Ed to a death scene, a badly decomposed woman whose apartment was piled with beer cans. The woman's gut was distended like a man's and her face was blackened from decomposition. Ed asked Tracy if she was strong enough to pick up the dead woman and she said: "No."

She just couldn't face the smell, a combination of rancidity really—like three-day-old damp laundry, rotting eggs, the pit of an ancient garbage can, sweat-stiffened socks at the bottom of a neglected gym locker. A mixture of all of those things, but more potent, pungent, concentrated.

When dealing with bad stinkers, newcomers to the coroner's office will sometimes put on a dust mask, but it doesn't really help. It's more a psychological thing, a barrier between the body and your nose and mouth. You can smear Vicks VapoRub on your upper lip or splash the inside of a surgical mask with wintergreen oil to overpower the smell, but it's impossible to entirely kill the odor of a bad stinker. Perhaps the only good thing about decomposed bodies is that no special care needs to be taken regarding their appearance—these bodies won't have open-casket funerals. Also, the smell may be the key that finally unlocks one of death investigation's most challenging riddles: time of death. Scientists in Tennessee are trying to build a device that could "smell" a corpse and determine how long it has been dead. The challenge is to correctly calculate the timing and rate at which a corpse releases various gases and vapors, and then factor in environmental variables such as temperature and humidity.

If you do this job a while, you just get used to the odor. It still smells bad, of course, but you get used to it, just like everything else. So Ed doesn't seem to hold Tracy's repugnance to the death smell against her. In the late afternoon, things get slow, and Ed launches into a story. He and another large deputy were carrying a corpse on a stretcher down a flight of stairs once when a stair broke under the weight of the other deputy. Both men stumbled, and Ed stepped backward to gain his balance, crashing into a wall behind him. The drywall and exterior siding gave way under the weight of Ed's considerable bulk, the corpse and the second deputy, and Ed found himself outside the house, still holding onto the stretcher. "We could have just taken him out the hole at that point," Ed says. "But I felt bad about it, so we brought him back inside and out the front door."

Ed has dozens of stories like this. Like the story of his busiest shift, years ago. People were dying everywhere that day. He collected nine bodies that shift, back and forth, back and forth, all evening long. He and Mike Chichwak worked in tandem, perfect efficiency, Mike writing up the case stories as Ed got the bodies into the cooler, and then they'd head out again. The last case was a suicide in the northern suburbs, a guy who'd attached a hose to his exhaust pipe and pumped the carbon monoxide into the car. The deputy coroners were running so hard that night that the cops and firefighters had waited two hours by the time they showed up. Ed was exhausted as he checked out the scene. Nothing unusual, typical suicide note, the guy depressed about being separated from his wife. So Ed got the body and left along with everybody else. Relatives later found something that the cops and firefighters and deputy coroners all missed: the lifeless body of the dead man's wife, in the back of a truck that was parked next to the suicide vehicle.

Ed got chewed out on that one.

A little before seven, the investigative office phones ring. Ed takes the call, and when he gets off, he asks if anybody knows where West Deer is.

Yeah, Tracy says. She went to high school there. She lives a couple miles away.

We got a call there, Ed says. A guy apparently shot himself.

Tracy is astonished. West Deer! All the people in Allegheny County, and a suicide call comes in from little bitty West Deer, a quiet place nobody knows unless they live there. Even Ed isn't sure where it is. He's probably never gotten a call from West Deer. Tracy asks Ed how old the victim was.

Twenty-one, Ed says.

Oh no, Tracy thinks. One year older than she is. What if she knows him from high school?

So halfway through the evening shift, Tracy heads back north toward home on the same highway her mom had taken to drive Tracy into the city four hours ago. After her accident the week before, Tracy is no longer driving herself. North of the city, more marinas and pleasure boats begin showing up on the Allegheny River. West Deer is a mixture of environments—countryside giving way to middle-class suburbia. Eleven thousand of Allegheny County's 1.2 million people live there. Gravel driveways marked by wagon wheels lead to houses set back from the roads and surrounded by woods. The dead man lived on a twisting country lane that runs along a ridge overlooking farmland. Newer houses are interspersed with ancient gray-slatted barns.

Tracy knows the road. A friend of hers lives on it, and it is only a few miles from her own home. The wagons park in front of a duplex with brown wood siding. Tracy and Carey follow Ed and Michael DeRosa up the wooden stairs and inside. Police show them to the dead man's bedroom, and there he is, lying on his bed, a gun in one hand, a telephone receiver in the other. Her heart in her throat, Tracy looks to see if she knows him.

Long pale lanky arms and legs, naked but for a black pair of briefs. A freckled face and neatly trimmed auburn hair—a fresh-faced suburban high school quarterback look that somehow clashes with black tattoos on his chest, stomach, and shoulder. Blood has run down his neck and pooled on his chest, drying and cracking like a dried-up lake bed.

Tracy doesn't know him.

A bit relieved, she looks around the room. A typical guy's room—messy, clothes on the floor. An air conditioner is propped in the window but silent, and the room is stifling hot. On the cluttered desk sits a computer, and the police point out what is on the screen, a poem. No suicide note, they say, just this poem by some long-ago writer named John Donne.

Ed prints it out for the case file, and Tracy reads it.

> *Death, be not proud, though some have called thee*
> *Mighty and dreadful, for thou art not so;*
> *For those, whom thou think'st thou dost overthrow,*
> *Die not, poor Death, nor yet canst thou kill me.*
> *From rest and sleep, which but thy pictures be,*
> *Much pleasure, then from thee much more must flow,*
> *And soonest our best men with thee do go,*

Rest of their bones, and soul's delivery.
Thou'rt slave to Fate, chance, kings, and desperate men,
And dost with poison, war, and sickness dwell,
And poppy, or charms can make us sleep as well,
And better than thy stroke; why swell'st thou then?
One short sleep past, we wake eternally,
And Death shall be no more; Death, thou shalt die.

County homicide detectives give Ed and DeRosa the story they've gotten from the dead man's roommate. Tracy saw the roommate on the way in, silent and sad. The night before, the roommate heard his friend come in around 11:00 p.m. Half an hour later, he heard his friend on the phone with his girlfriend, arguing as usual. Then the roommate heard a sharp sound and thought it was his friend throwing the phone against the wall. He went to bed. After work the next day, he went into his roommate's bedroom.

Ed and DeRosa inspect the body. The police haven't touched him, of course. The dead man's jaw is slack and bloody—he apparently shot himself in the mouth. It is difficult to tell where the exit wound is, but the cops have found a hole in the thin wall behind the dead man's head. The bullet penetrated into the other side of the duplex. Fortunately, the couple who live there were on vacation. Unfortunately, that means someone will have to come back later to retrieve the bullet.

Ed and DeRosa know that homicide and suicide by gunshot can look an awful lot alike, which means a homicide can be covered up by faking suicide. Therefore, all the investigation routines must be done with care. Properly bagging and swabbing the hands is crucial in apparent gunshot suicides—if the hands don't bear gunshot residue in the right places, it might be homicide. Deputy coroners note and document the angles of bullet holes and the position of the body to make sure they match up with the autopsy findings. Eighty percent of suicide victims shoot themselves in the head, and most of those put the gun in their mouths.

An empty bullet casing lies on the dead man's chest, and the deputies bag it. The body's lividity pattern is consistent with the position of the body, indicating that he hasn't been moved. He is stiff as a flagpole, in full rigor mortis, which means he's been dead for at least a few hours. The county homicide detectives gingerly unclasp the dead man's stiff hand from the gun, a .40-caliber Smith & Wesson semi-automatic pistol. The deputy coroners slide paper bags over his hands to preserve any evidence on them and snap rubber bands over his wrists to hold the bags in place.

The police point out another item on the dead man's desk, a girl's photo. The dead man's girlfriend, the roommate has told the police, the one he was arguing with before he shot himself. The dead man's wallet contains more photos of the same girl.

Tracy takes a look. Unlike the dead man, the girl in the photo looks familiar. She looks like someone Tracy knows from Deer Lakes High School, a girl a couple classes above her. Tracy can't say for sure, but the probable coincidence is enough to unsettle her.

Back at the office, the dead man's father calls. Police came to his house and told him to call the coroner's office. Ed breaks the news. Later in the conversation, the father tells Ed that his son suffered from mood swings in high school, but he thought that he'd gotten past that phase. He says he thought his son had matured.

A recent study performed by the coroner's office and doctors from Western Psychiatric Institute and Clinic in Pittsburgh show that the three factors most likely to increase the odds of a male teenager killing himself are mental illness, intoxication, and access to a loaded gun. Young men are more likely to use guns and succeed in killing themselves; young women are more likely to overdose on drugs but survive. "Attempters" typically act on impulse; those who succeed have generally planned the act and have told a friend. Youths who commit suicide have often shown symptoms of mental illness for years, but parents may mistakenly consider these signs as normal mood swings.

The year before, fourteen males under the age of twenty-five killed themselves in Allegheny County, eight with guns. Ninety-nine of the county's 136 suicides were white males. That year, 1999, suicides were more likely to happen on weekdays than weekends, in summer months rather than winter months, November being the exception with the highest number of suicides, sixteen.

That year, people killed themselves by drowning, drug overdoses, gunfire, hanging, jumping from high places, and cutting themselves. One walked in front of a train. Guns and drugs were by far the most common methods. Most people did it at home, although a few chose more public places like parks, emergency rooms, and cemeteries. Bad health was the most common suicide motive, followed by relationship difficulties, job or money problems and criminal troubles.

The next day, the young suicide victim is stretched out tall on the autopsy table in front of Tracy, looking just the same as he had the night before. Dr. Leon Rozin sketches the young man's tattoos onto the body diagram sheet, and the autopsy techs play their usual height-weight game, guessing that the dead man is seventy-three inches tall. They stretch the tape. "Seventy-five inches!" the tech reports, surprised.

Tracy still feels a little shocked. All week she had braced herself for her upcoming Monday night shift, the gore, the stinkers. But not this. She hadn't predicted this—a guy, one year older than herself, killing himself in her neighborhood.

The autopsy techs, Patti and Don, pause in their preparations for the autopsy to check out the dead man's tattoos more closely. His shoulder bears the idealized image of a horse's head, mane flowing. The other tattoos seem less innocent, particularly the one that includes three black skulls with the word DIABLO above them.

Patti especially gets a kick out of the tattooed thunderbolts that radiate from the dead man's belly button. Just back from a Las Vegas vacation, she's in a good mood. "I want to get one of these," Patti says, pointing at the thunderbolts. "On my butt."

Carey feels comfortable enough this week to join in on the joking. She points at the DIABLO tattoo. "How do you decide to get this particular tattoo?" she says. "Do you pick it out of a book or something?"

Tracy grins with the others, but she feels a little uneasy.

To work around death, Mike Chichwak believes, you must have a sense of humor. Some jokes will be at the expense of the corpses—jokes about how they smell, how they look, how they're too fat or too ugly. And everybody joins in, although there's a difference between the manner of the veterans and the novices. Young uniform cops are typically less familiar with working around dead bodies and often are a trifle uneasy. Young cops seem to make jokes to stifle that discomfort. Interns do it to fit in. The veterans—the deputy coroners and homicide detectives—make jokes out of habit.

Psychologists have surveyed funeral directors and found that they are very defensive about morgue humor. One 1986 study concluded that "Funeral directors do not joke, or do not admit to joking about death." Another study concluded that morticians were less humorous. However, a sociologist who had done more in-depth interviews with morticians found that they did indeed use humor to cope with death and the stigma associated with their profession. It just took a while before they were comfortable enough to start telling jokes to outsiders.

Funny things happen at death scenes. Not long ago, one deputy coroner solemnly pushing a loaded gurney through a Holiday Inn lobby fell down, accidentally knocking the gurney over and pulling the body on top of him in front of all the hotel guests. The other day, someone pointed out how a corpse in rigor seemed to be giving the autopsy technician who'd just cut him open a stiff middle finger. Everybody had a good laugh. The most brutal scenes can bring out the comedian in everybody. Deputy coroners still joke about the severed head that belonged to a murdered RN—they call her the "head nurse." Even when you feel bad about it, as Tiffani sometimes does, it's hard not to crack up.

Sometimes the mood of a death scene transforms in an instant. A few months ago, Tiffani and an intern were working a suicide case, a middle-aged suburban man who started his car in his garage and lay down next to the exhaust pipe to breathe in the carbon monoxide fumes. As firefighters dispersed the fumes in the garage, the intern, a young college student, formulated playful theories about the "real story" behind the death. Maybe the kids staged the suicide, he said. "Sounds fishy to me," he said. A few moments later, a woman drove up and saw the ambulance and coroner's wagon blocking the driveway.

She jumped out of her Jeep, a stricken look on her face. The cops and deputy coroners and firefighters stopped talking. A policewoman approached the newcomer.

"Who is it?" the woman demanded. "Who!"

The officer told her.

"No . . . No!" the woman shrieked. In a strangled, determined voice, emphasizing each word, she stated: "Not my dad. . . . No . . . *Oh!* . . . Not him, no." Her protestations trailed off into a scream. "Oh *God*, no! *No!*"

She crumpled against a telephone pole, and the policewoman reached for her. Everybody else seemed immobilized, including the intern. Behind the open door of the coroner's wagon, the young college student stood perfectly still, stunned by the ferocity of the woman's grief, as if he might catch it if he moved.

Sometimes in this job you feel like a personal carrier of grief—you spread it everywhere. Some cases are almost unbearably sad—child deaths, of course. Some make you angry, such as when the mother or father are crying and grieving at the scene, but then you get back to the office and find evidence of abuse.

But the worst are the ones with no one to blame, so there's no anger to ease your sadness. Like the time a father found his baby asphyxiated by the safety belt of a high chair. The pathologist determined after an autopsy that the father had attached the safety straps the wrong way. The deputy coroner who investigated that case didn't have the heart to tell the grieving father the whole truth, so he kept quiet.

The job has different effects on different people. Bob Keys began working as a deputy coroner in 1983. The next year, the *Pittsburgh Post-Gazette* ran a feature story about deputy coroners and quoted Bob on the difficulty of investigating child deaths. "You never get used it. You learn to tolerate it, but you never get used to it. You deal with it, that's all. You must appear professional. You've got to keep your emotions inside."

Bob never did get used to it. A trim blond man with hooded, weary-looking eyes, he was fascinated by death investigation, but haunted by some cases. In 1986, a friend of his was raped and killed in another county, and Bob quit working the coroner's office a year later, unable to face more destruction of life. But he returned to the job and eventually learned how to separate the work from the rest of his life. He learned how the particularly tragic cases could help him appreciate his own life more keenly.

Some deputy coroners, like Tiffani Hunt, find this job difficult because there sometimes seems to be no upside. Other jobs involve death and tragedy—firefighting, nursing, paramedical work—but the people who do those jobs draw conviction from the idea that they are helping people. Deputy coroners find their jobs interesting, but it doesn't always feel like they're helping anybody directly. Sure, they identify public health hazards and help catch killers. Sometimes they can help survivors or at least treat them with kindness. But most of the time, the job consists of dealing with people who are beyond help.

Now Bob Keys is in his late thirties and is a senior deputy, which means he doesn't have to work death scenes anymore. Along with other duties, he runs the office's educational programs, giving tours of the coroner's office at least once a week. The office receives cops, lawyers, and reporters on a daily basis. Homicide detectives often come to watch autopsies, and even they, who are accustomed to dead bodies, can find them jarring. A month earlier, a steel-worker in one of Pittsburgh's few remaining mills collapsed and died on the job. On the postmortem table, his pot belly jutted like Mount Washington toward the fluorescent lights. A county police detective watching the autopsy shuddered at the thick layer of yellow fat the techs had to cut through to get to the abdominal organs. He looked down at his own belly.

"I hope I don't look like that," the detective said. "Makes you want to go out and get some exercise."

In recent weeks, other visitors have included a batch of paramedic students from Iceland, two criminology students from Nebraska, an unannounced group on an architectural tour of Pittsburgh, assistant district attorneys and assistant public defenders who came for a rape-homicide seminar, and several deputy coroners from nearby counties who came for coroner's school.

Bob is most enthusiastic about the underage drinking program. Twice a month, a group of teenagers who have been convicted of alcohol violations tour the coroner's office as part of their sentence. Bob takes them up to the court-room, where he tries to get them to open up about their drinking and drug use. Then he gives them statistics and data about alcohol and drugs. Then they head downstairs to watch an autopsy. Some of the kids are openly fearful, and ask Bob where they will go if they need to throw up. Others treat it as a joke, swaggering and making jokes about how hungry they are. Bob accepts either attitude, asking only that the kids remove their baseball caps during the autopsy and act respectful in front of the bodies. "Look at it in a scientific kind of way," he tells them. "These bodies are evidence."

Without fail, even the boldest kids are disconcerted when they see a body opened up for the first time. Some can barely stand to watch. They pull their shirts up over their noses and grimace at the sound of the bone saw. The autopsy techs get in on the show. "Here's all those beers and hamburgers," one tech says, pointing at a yellow fat pad. "This is what it looks like." As the kids trail out of the room after the autopsy, another tech calls out: "All right, guys. We don't want to see you here again."

Afterward, some kids are silent. Others say the experience is surprisingly similar to gutting a deer. Usually, one kid will be hooked. After the initial shock fades, he'll watch the autopsy closely, asking questions. Afterward, Bob will single that one out, urging him to study science or even apply for an internship at the coroner's office.

Others have an entirely different reaction. Two weeks ago, one boy leaned over to another during the autopsy and said: "There couldn't be a worse job than this. Who would do this job?"

Not everybody can do this job. But people who don't have strong stomachs don't get into it in the first place, so that's not usually the problem. Certainly new deputy coroners have to adjust to bad stinkers or bloody scenes, stuff you don't normally see in everyday life. Maybe they order vegetarian for a while. But sooner or later, they're popping their spaghetti bolognese frozen dinners into the autopsy lounge microwave just like everybody else. You get used to it.

Other parts of the job prove more challenging in the long run. Five years ago, a nine-month-old died at Children's Hospital in Pittsburgh after a gastrointestinal operation. Two deputy coroners drove to the hospital to pick up the body and the case history. Hospital officials told the deputy coroners that the mother was in bad condition and not ready to give up the body. The deputies returned to the coroner's office, where an administrator ordered them to return to the hospital and get the body. One of the deputy coroners, a former nurse who had worked at the coroner's office less than a year, repeatedly refused to go back for the body and was suspended without pay for three days. She has since left the coroner's office.

Not everybody can do this job.

If you can't bear tragedy with a certain level of detachment, then you probably won't last long. The trick is to be detached without growing callous. On difficult cases, Ed Strimlan reminds himself that he is not to blame for the victim's misfortune, and that he can best help by doing a good investigation. Mike Chichwak tries to display empathy, hoping that an understanding attitude will help people ease a little more smoothly into the grief process. But both men leave their work at the office.

So does Dr. Bennet Omalu. The job has made him a better Christian, he says, more aware of life's fragility and blessings.

Last month, Bennet dissected a fetus. The coroner's office investigates a handful of fetal cases each year, only when the death might have been caused by criminal actions. Bennet opened the fetus himself, rather than having one of the autopsy techs do it. He tried lying the tiny body flat on the table, like other corpses, but it shifted around too much. Finally, he just picked it up in one gloved hand and worked the scalpel with the other. The fingerlike limbs dangled down over his hand. He found that the infant had suffered from fetal distress over a period of days or weeks, which meant that the mother had likely suffered no sudden trauma that led to the miscarriage. Nobody was to blame.

During the procedure, the autopsy room was quiet, but not uncomfortably so. People spoke in casual tones, but they did not chatter as usual about trivialities. Nobody turned off the radio. When a technician from the histology lab came into the room, Bennet looked up and smiled. "You were once like this, remember."

The histology tech laughed once. "Yes, I was once like that, but I don't remember," he said.

But the tech had not understood. Bennet's comment wasn't a joking question. It was a reminder.

Don and Patti work on the young suicide as Tracy and Carey watch. The interns tell them the story about the suicide call, and everyone shakes their heads at the idea of killing yourself over girlfriend trouble.

"You know she'll have a new boyfriend next week," Patti predicts.

She pulls the paper bags off the suicide's hands.

"His hands were bagged because he shot himself?" Tracy asks.

"Yes," Patti says. "To protect the powder residue."

Patti retrieves the atomic absorption case, which looks like a plastic sewing kit. She takes small cotton stick swabs moistened with nitric acid, dabs the man's palms and the backs of his hands, and puts the swabs in labeled containers. Two swabs are used for the backs of the hands and two for the palms. Technicians will test the swabs for the presence of lead, antimony, and barium. The amount of residue and the location of it on the hands can lead a pathologist—or a judge—to different interpretations. Typically, the cloud of residue settles on the back of a shooter's hand, not the palm. Thus, if the backs of the hands contain residue, that may mean the dead person committed suicide. If the victim's palms contain residue, that may mean the victim was struggling with the shooter over the gun when it discharged.

Bullet entry wounds can help pathologists narrow down the type of gun and ammunition used and the distance from which the gun was fired. In almost all suicides, the gun muzzle is touching the skin, which leaves a black ring around the entrance wound where the gunpowder and gases discharged from the gun barrel and scorched the skin. If an uncovered entrance wound bears no powder marks at all, the gun barrel likely was more than a foot and a half away from the skin, and investigators may start thinking homicide. Pathologists can tell from the markings whether the gun was jammed hard against the skin or held loosely, whether the barrel was pointed directly at the body or angled. Suicide victims tend to shoot themselves in the same areas— below the chin, in the temple, in the mouth—and unusual angles or non-contact wounds are scrutinized carefully. The previous fall, Dr. Shaun Ladham autopsied a man who had shot himself near the back of the head at such an awkward angle that if it weren't for the suicide note and the victim's advanced cancer, he might have begun to wonder.

Every so often, suicide will disguise itself as homicide. Multiple gunshot wounds usually mean murder, but even that is not a sure thing. About fifteen years ago, a man shot himself in the head three times, grazing his forehead and shooting himself in the cheeks before firing the last bullet through his temple and into his brain. And every so often, a pathologist will come across a faked homicide of the kind described by Sir Arthur Conan Doyle in his Sherlock Holmes story, "The Problem of Thor Bridge." In that story, a woman shoots herself with a gun that is attached by a string to a large stone that hangs over a bridge railing above a river. In a recent copycat case, a man tried to improve upon the Thor Bridge method by putting the revolver inside a plastic sandwich bag, probably so he wouldn't get gunshot residue on his hands. Police might have tagged the case a homicide but for one snafu: the gun-rope-weight device got snagged before it fell into the water.

Next, Patti cuts off the suicide's black underwear. The lividity is so pronounced that the elastic band of the underwear has left a paler stripe around his midsection, with tiny dead-white words that read RALPH LAUREN where the embroidered brand name had pressed itself into the skin. Patti hoses the body down and scrapes off the dried blood, then holds open the slack jaw for Dr. Leon Rozin to look inside and probe for fractures.

After noting the placement of the entry wound in the mouth, Rozin fingers the back of the man's head, looking for an exit wound. He can't find it immediately and wonders aloud if the bullet is still inside the skull.

"The bullet went through the wall behind him, so there should be an exit wound," Carey offers, less intimidated by Rozin this week.

Rozin does locate the wound in the back of the skull. Sis and Don help Patti roll the dead man onto his side. Patti holds him there with a hand on his hip while Don shaves the exit wound with a scalpel for the clean photos.

Don tugs the dead man onto his back again. "Boy, he's a slippery son of a gun," the tech mutters. The suicide's slack head falls off the cutting block and thumps heavily against the table, hard skull on steel. Watching, Tracy winces and breathes: "Oooh."

Now, the suicide's face is red with fresh blood. Facing down for a while got the blood moving again. After pulling on a splash mask, Patti brandishes a fresh scalpel, ready to make the Y cut. Once again, just like last week, Tracy has to leave. She still can't watch the cutting, not yet.

Carey hangs around, watching Patti cut the body open and extract fluids and organs. When they ask her to take organ weights, she smiles and slides behind a wooden stand. "Got it," she says. She's learning the routine.

Sis cuts the scalp. As difficult as it was to find the exit wound, under the scalp it's an obvious bloody mess. The bullet punched out a neat hole in the skull, just big enough to stick the tip of a pinkie finger through.

Rozin seems to have noticed Carey's interest in the autopsy proceedings. He calls her over to look at the exit wound. You can tell it's an exit wound and not a bullet fired to the back of the head, he says, because the opening on the outside of his skull is bigger than the opening on the inside of his skull. Carey is having a hard time deciphering the doctor's accent, but she nods. Rozin opens the dead man's mouth for Carey to look inside. "Usually, when people fire guns in their mouths, the palate is fractured," he explains. "Here, the hard palate is intact." If the doctor keeps finding oddities like this, too many deviations from the norm, the pathologist will begin considering explanations other than suicide. But right now, the facts that the body is offering seem to line up with the scene investigation and the story given by the dead man's roommate.

If Rozin is treating Carey with respect, Don still seems to be testing her. He fires information at her, not pausing to give her a chance to get it all down. The bullet, he says, perforated the soft palate, the tip of the tongue, and the base of the skull, behind and to the left of the sphenoid sinus. When he continues, Carey politely interrupts him, her pen continuing to scribble, and asks him how to spell sphenoid. After that, Don slows down.

The techs bring out another body, a stinker. A bad stinker. A couple of deputy coroners hanging out in the autopsy room retreat to the lounge and close the door. But Carey stays and writes down the information. The dead woman is weighed and measured. She's five feet two inches tall and weighs 172 pounds. Carey, who is also five-two, looks down at her own petite frame. "That's 172 pounds on me," she says in amazement.

Tracy comes back in the room, then leaves again as the smell of the rotting corpse spreads.

"The smell doesn't bother you?" Patti asks Carey. "Everyone else ran out."

Carey just laughs. More than blood or awful sights, she'd been worried that she wouldn't be able to handle the smells. She knows now that she can.

"Tell you what," Don grunts. "She just might win the cast-iron nose award."

Cut open and emptied out, the dead man lies still on the autopsy table. Sis closes his slack jaw with a latexed finger, then lets go and the jaw drops open again. Sis sighs and, under her breath, says: "Young kid like this."

Patti hefts the red plastic biohazard bag full of organs, twists it to get rid of the air and ties it off. She jams the bag inside the stomach cavity and places the rib plate back on the chest. She folds the flesh back over where it belongs, the insides disappear, and the anatomy-lesson body becomes a man again— a kid, really.

Patti cuts a length of twine, threads the needle, and begins sewing the body back together, the red biohazard bag visible between the edges of skin. Then she carefully fits the skullcap back onto the cranium and sews the scalp back together too.

SEVEN

THE TV TEAM

The phone rings, and Michael DeRosa takes the call. Forty-year-old female, dead in Ben Avon. Alone in the investigative office, DeRosa goes searching for a partner. In the entrance hall, he runs into Ed Strimlan. "Want to take a ride?" DeRosa asks.

"Whatcha got?" Ed asks.

"A big girl," DeRosa says.

They head downstairs to the wagons. Just before they pull out, Ed remembers something. He jumps out of his wagon and calls upstairs on the garage phone. Mike Chichwak picks up, and Ed says he and DeRosa are going on a call and could he track down the camera crew, the guys from MSNBC? Mike says OK.

When Ed hangs up, DeRosa says: "You didn't have to do that."

"I know," Ed says. "I just don't want anybody bitching at me tomorrow."

Ed doesn't tell DeRosa this, but the truth is, he doesn't mind being on camera, in the public eye. He's good at speaking about his job—funny and knowledgeable and articulate. Unlike many deputy coroners, he is friendly with some local reporters. He enjoys giving drunk-driving lectures during the mock car crashes the coroner's office stages at high schools during prom season. He really liked being a guest speaker in a course on death and dying at the local community college. He thinks he might pursue teaching further—maybe a night class on anatomy or physiology—after he switches to the day shift at the end of the month. He's looking forward to it.

The MSNBC producer and cameraman come down. The producer, a lanky, goateed man named Trent Gillies, is in Pittsburgh for the week, shooting a one-hour installment of a documentary series called *Crime Files*. The deputy coroners are under orders to page Gillies in his room at the Marriott before they go on calls, but this hasn't always worked out. Gillies missed a good case a couple days earlier when a woman stole a van and then, fleeing police, smashed into a truck, killing the driver. And the day they were supposed to shoot the autopsy room, the pathologist refused to be taped.

So Gillies is eager to take advantage of Ed's cooperation. He cut short an interview with the serology lab to come on this call. The juiciest case he's gotten so far this week, a man beaten to death in a homeless camp on the South Side slopes, also involved Ed.

Gillies instructs the cameraman to get a shot of Ed sitting in the driver's seat of the wagon. The photographer props the camera on his shoulder and aims it through the passenger window. Ed needs no prompting to ignore the camera and just stare through the windshield of the idling wagon, as if he's pondering the case ahead. But he can't quite suppress a faint smile, breaking one of his own rules for dealing with the media. Ed has two on-camera rules: never look straight at the lens and never smile. Although it's unnatural on this job to keep a straight face. It's unnatural not to joke around with the homicide detectives at death scenes, because funny stuff happens. But Ed is media-savvy enough to understand how bad it looks on television.

The tape rolls for a few seconds, and then the cameraman looks at Gillies. "You want to ask him anything?"

"What do we know so far about this case?" Gillies asks quickly, in sonorous television tones.

"We know we have a forty-year-old lady in her apartment, apparently with no past medical history," Ed says smoothly. "So we're going to go out to the scene and find out what we have and go from there."

Gillies thanks him and says they're just waiting for the sound technician before they can take off for the scene. Ed nods. He's getting used to the inconvenience. During the homeless-camp homicide investigation, Ed and Tiffani had been accompanied by an administrator, an intern, and the three MSNBC people. (A photographer from the *Pittsburgh Post-Gazette* took advantage of the crowd and ducked under the police tape, too.) That crime scene was located on a steep and rocky hillside, cluttered with makeshift bunks, bags, and clothes. The dead man had been dragged and hidden in a bed of crown vetch, and the rapacious ground cover had already begun entangling the body. Searching for a TV-appropriate topic of death-scene chitchat, Ed gave the homicide detectives an impromptu lecture on the history and unique qualities of crown vetch. (Ed knows horticulture from his years at Trax Farm.) When it came time to get the body up the hill, the coroner's office administrator suggested the deputies use block and tackle, a last-resort method for retrieving bodies from cliffsides and mines. In this case, Ed suspected the suggestion had less to do with practicality and more to do with providing good tape for the TV crew, and he refused. A few minutes later, the lurking *Post-Gazette* photographer snapped a picture of Ed, Tiffani, and a homicide detective lugging the bagged body up the hillside. At the top of the hill, the MSNBC crew stuck a camera in Ed's face, but the big man was still wheezing so he waved them off. He gave them the rundown a few minutes later.

The coroner's wagons, followed by the TV team's beige van, head north up the Ohio River to a leafy town called Ben Avon. The caravan pulls up in front of a yellow-painted brick row house with a green awning over the porch. The cameraman hustles over to film Ed grabbing a camera and blue latex gloves from the back of the wagon. Then the cameraman scurries up the sidewalk to film Ed walking up to the house. Ed makes sure not to look at the camera, acting as if everything's normal.

On the porch, he consults with three local police officers. They don't want the camera inside. So Ed heads inside the house and upstairs. In a hot, cramped bedroom, a short, fat woman lies on the floor at the end of the bed.

Yellow purge runs from her nose. Stacks of clothing fill the room, which smells like urine.

Ed sees two fans in the windows. They had been running, one of the cops says, but a breaker must have blown. Ed takes a closer look at the dead woman. He sees no overt signs of violence. She's wearing a gown and underwear. When Ed lifts the gown for the liver stick, he sees an unnatural bulge in her stomach. The lump is shockingly large—the size of a bowler hat. Not pregnancy, it is shaped differently. An internal growth of some sort. It certainly could be what killed her. They'd find out tomorrow, during the autopsy. But for now, with no signs of foul play, this is going to be a scoop and run; DeRosa is already downstairs interviewing the cops. No intrigue. Too bad for the TV crew.

The room is too cramped to put the stretcher by the woman's side or to do a two-man lift. Ed positions the bag as close as he can to the woman, then grabs her arm and flips her onto the bag all by himself. When she's strapped in, Ed grabs the bottom end of the body bag and DeRosa and a beefy local cop take the other for the trip down the stairs.

The TV crew tapes the men coming out of the house and stowing away the body in the wagon. Then Gillies and the cameraman approach Ed for the rundown. Breathing lightly, his hands on his hips, Ed says it appears to be a natural death. He hitches his belt and clasps his hands under his belly. "This kind of case happens more than any other," he says.

Gillies looks disappointed.

Ed doesn't know it, but he's caught in the middle of what one TV reviewer will later call prime-time television's "forensic phase." This summer, CBS is developing a new dramatic series called *CSI: Crime Scene Investigation*, the *Quincy, M.E.* for a new generation. *CSI* will prove to be a hit, followed the next year by numerous dramas and real-life forensics shows.

TV may have been plunging into a forensic phase, but fans of the science have enjoyed the exploits of fictional and real-life medical detectives for more than a century. Take Sherlock Holmes, who could distinguish between 140 different types of tobacco ash, could tell whether a man was lazy by looking at scrape marks on his boot heel, and could roughly determine a person's age through handwriting analysis. More scientifically, Holmes beat corpses in a dissecting-room in order to "verify how far bruises may be produced after death," and solved crimes by using plaster casts of footprints. When Watson meets him for the first time, Holmes is rejoicing over his latest discovery—a chemical test for bloodstains. ("Why, man, it's the most practical medico-legal discovery for years," Holmes cries.)

Holmes's creator, Sir Arthur Conan Doyle, based his fictional detective on Dr. Joseph Bell, a Scottish surgeon renowned for his powers of observation and deduction. On occasion, Doyle exercised detective skills himself. Once he exonerated a man convicted of swindling by proving it was a case of mistaken identity, and another time proved that evidence had been manufactured against a man wrongly convicted of maiming animals. Over the years, Doyle grew weary of Holmes and obsessed with the idea of communicating with the dead (he claimed to have had conversations with many great deceased men, including Joseph Conrad). But Holmes was such a hit that Doyle grudgingly churned out the detective mysteries until late in life.

In a period of urbanization and rising crime rates, readers were attracted to Holmes's ability to scrutinize a murder scene and summon arcane scraps of knowledge to condemn a killer. Holmes almost always knew more than the police and was always eager to point that out. In the following passage from the first Sherlock Holmes story, "A Study in Scarlet," Holmes has just given a death scene the once-over with a magnifying glass and a measuring tape.

"I'll tell you one thing which may help you in the case," [Holmes] continued, turning to the two detectives. "There has been murder done, and the murderer was a man. He was more than six feet high, was in the prime of life, had small feet for his height, wore coarse, square-toed boots and smoked a Trichinopoly cigar. He came here with his victim in a four-wheeled cab, which was drawn by a horse with three old shoes and one new one on his off fore-leg. In all probability the murderer had a florid face, and the finger-nails of his right hand were remarkably long. These are only a few indications, but they may assist you."

Though not a forensic pathologist, Holmes served as a prototype for nearly all the medical detectives who followed him in print and on-screen. Dr. Edmund Locard, who built the first forensic laboratory in France in 1910, studied Doyle's novels as if they were textbooks. "I hold that a police expert, or an examining magistrate, would not find it a waste of time to read Doyle's novels," he later wrote. Ever since then, whether real-life or fictional, forensic experts have been portrayed—or portrayed themselves—as Sherlockian: condescending, all-knowing, and nearly infallible.

The most famous of the early medical detectives was the British forensic pathologist, Sir Bernard Spilsbury, whose name first spread when he testified in a high-profile murder trial in 1910, establishing the identity of a dead woman from an old surgical scar and some tufts of hair. After surveying crime scenes, Spilsbury often gave sweeping statements about the crime and perpetrator that were Sherlockian in scope. Much as they loved the Holmes stories, the public loved Spilsbury's dramatics, the triumph of scientific observation over crime. His name packed courtrooms.

Spilsbury was not the only one to adopt the Holmes persona. Many pathologists over the years wrote memoirs, some dour, others dramatic, but all tending toward noirish titles and chapters that sounded like stories from pulp crime magazines. "The Strangling of Chrissie Gall." " 'Acid Bath' Haigh and the Undissolved Gallstone." "The Career Girl Murders." Sir Sydney Smith, a Scottish pathologist in the first half of the twentieth century, was a protégé of Bell and rival of Spilsbury. In his memoir, "Mostly Murder," Smith describes his analysis of three bones, sounding a lot like Holmes:

. . . The police asked me only to determine whether or not they were human. After looking at the bones, I was able to tell them more than that.

"They are the bones of a young woman," I reported. "She was short and slim. Aged between twenty-three and twenty-five when she died, which was at least three months ago. She had probably had at least one pregnancy, perhaps more. Her left leg was shorter than her right, and she walked with a pronounced limp.

Probably she had polio when a child. She was killed by a shotgun loaded with home-made slugs, fired in an upward direction from a range of about three yards. The killer was standing, or sitting, in front of her, and slightly to her left. She was not killed outright, but died about seven to ten days later, probably from septic peritonitis due to the shooting."

Modern forensic pathologists have continued the tradition of writing self-congratulatory memoirs about their most intriguing cases.

Perhaps the most prolific of all modern forensic pathologists is Allegheny County's own Dr. Cyril Wecht, who has written some thirty books. In addition to professional tomes, he has penned three popular forensics books, which explore a variety of investigations that he has either headed or reviewed later, some high-profile, others not. (In his 1993 book, *Cause of Death*, Wecht quotes the "great" Sherlock Holmes: "Once you have eliminated the impossible, whatever remains, however improbable, must be the answer.") Wecht's books also highlight his Holmes-like inclination for theories that go against conventional wisdom. In *Grave Secrets*, Wecht reviews the evidence and theorizes that *two* people, not one, likely killed Nicole Brown Simpson and Ron Goldman. (He doesn't rule out O.J.)

The Simpson trial heightened the profile of forensic specialists even more, and exposed a riveted nation to the intricacies of blood-spatter analysis and DNA. Wecht repeatedly weighed in on the O.J. Simpson murder trial on shows such as *Rivera Live* and *Nightline*. He is friends with many of the defense-team figures, including Johnnie Cochran (who came to Pittsburgh to campaign for Wecht in 1999, a move that many agreed probably did not help Wecht in his losing bid for county executive), F. Lee Bailey (who wrote a foreword for *Cause of Death*), and Barry Scheck. (Some deputy coroners don't like Scheck, the lawyer who bullied the LAPD criminologist during cross-examination and helped discredit the prosecution's DNA evidence. On occasion, when Scheck has called the Allegheny County Coroner's Office for Wecht, he's been put on hold for longer than necessary.) Although Simpson's defense team ripped apart the prosecution's forensic specialists, the trial gave the country a deeper understanding of crime-scene investigation and forensic pathology. (If Simpson and Goldman had died in Allegheny County, the results might have been very different. For one thing, the coroner's office would have been an immediate and integral part of the investigation. Police would not have touched the bodies until the deputy coroners and pathologists got there. In Los Angeles, no medical examiner was summoned for hours, and crucial evidence was trampled and lost.)

The Simpson case was a watershed moment for an exclusive group of forensic pathologists and criminologists who jet all over the country and world to consult on cases. Usually these are cases in which the killer or killed have money. But sometimes they'll take a case for free if it might yield an intriguing chapter in a book, land them a spot on *Dateline*, or if it simply looks interesting enough. These forensic experts swap vials of blood, autopsy reports, and crime scene photographs. They huddle together over exhumed bodies in remote graveyards or in hospital pathology rooms, debating the intricacies of gunpowder residue or blood-alcohol reports. In other cases they examine the evidence separately and face off in court, presenting different interpretations, and then they meet afterward for dinner and backslapping. They write glowing introductions for each other's books and shake their heads together over the bungling of small-town homicide investigators.

Wecht is a charter member of this group, most of whom became acquainted in the '60s and '70s. He gets involved with high-profile cases through requests from attorneys or fellow members of the forensic elite. They call him at the office or at home (his home number is listed in the telephone directory), and he always calls back. Wecht consults on about two hundred outside cases a year. His clients send him autopsy records, photographs, microscopic slides, and deposition transcripts, from which he draws his conclusions.

Other members of Wecht's circle include Dr. Thomas Noguchi, the longtime "coroner to the stars" in Los Angeles who wrote about his investigations of the deaths of Robert Kennedy, Marilyn Monroe, and Natalie Wood.

Noguchi, who rarely hid his relish for the spotlight and intrigue, was forced out of office in 1982. Dr. Michael Baden, a medical examiner in New York City for more than twenty-five years, has built a career of explaining forensic pathology in books and on HBO's *Autopsy*. His biggest consultations include the Simpson case and the JFK assassination, and his clashes with authority figures are legendary in his field. There are a few others, criminalist Dr. Henry Lee and blood-spatter expert Herb MacDonell among them.

Just as the early 1900s had its Holmes/Spilsbury duo, the last decade of the century had its fictional as well as real-life medical detectives. On-screen, medical examiners and coroners began showing up more frequently, often on cop shows. In a 1999 movie titled *The Bone Collector*, Denzel Washington plays a paralyzed forensic specialist who investigates a series of killings with the help of a police officer played by Angelina Jolie. Patricia Cornwell, author of a series of crime novels starring a fictional medical examiner in Virginia, has written at least six of the twenty-five best-selling mystery books ever, according to a 1996 *USA Today* list. Cornwell was a crime reporter for the *Charlotte Observer* who later worked for the chief medical examiner's office in Virginia. Her darkly atmospheric books are full of autopsy tables, scalpels, and yellow crime-scene tape.

And then there is *CSI* and its main character, Gil Grissom, who has proven to be the most Sherlockian death investigator yet. Both Holmes and Grissom are unmarried, middle-aged, male scientists. Like Holmes, Grissom is oblivious to fields of endeavor that don't relate to criminology. (In this regard, Grissom may be even more single-minded than Holmes, who at least enjoys cocaine and plays the violin expertly; Grissom's only hobby is entomology—the study of insects, which can be used in forensic investigations.) Like Holmes, Grissom is steeped in arcana that proves useful in investigations. (When a dead man is found to have traces of uranium in his wounds, Grissom informs a lab tech that the radioactive mineral was used years ago as a color enhancer in paints. As it turns out, the killer beat the victim to death with an antique garden gnome.) Like Holmes, Grissom spouts maxims about the philosophy of crime investigation. ("A butterfly flaps its wings in Brazil, we get a hurricane off the coast of

Florida—chaos theory," Grissom muses during one confusing case. "Random events, the wholesale rejection of linear thought.")

CSI was the number-one new show in its first season. The show is fun, every case intriguing. Crimes are recreated in hazy flashbacks as the camera appears to dive into a corpse, tunneling through lungs and livers to show the path of a bullet. The methods that Grissom and his team use to solve crimes are typically elaborate. The technicians sprinkle blood on running chainsaws to see how it spatters and wrap dead pigs in blankets to see how long it takes for flies to invade the skin.

But its appeal may have deeper roots. Like the Sherlock Holmes stories, the show is comforting. The crime techs are experts who regularly work late into the night. They pull out gee-whiz technological gadgets with names like electronic polymer sensor proboscis and electrothermal atomizers. They go to extravagant lengths, such as extracting the stomach contents of a Silphib beetle and running tests to determine if it contains a victim's DNA. Toxicological tests come back from the lab in hours, not weeks. Unlike most cop shows and certainly unlike the Simpson trial, *CSI* portrays science as infallible, a comforting antidote to the uncertainty of crime.

An hour after returning with Ed, the TV crew gets another chance. Mike Chichwak gets a call from city homicide: a bone found in Bloomfield, possibly human. Mike gets off the phone and says: "A lady at the scene apparently says it looks like a *female* bone! And she's a nurse!" The TV people are nowhere to be seen at the moment, so everyone cracks up, laughing at the idea of a non-expert identifying a bone as male or female by just looking at it.

Just as Mike is pulling out of the garage to head to the scene solo, the TV crew's van pulls up behind him. Gillies jumps out and asks Mike what's going on.

"Someone found some bones," Mike says. "Want to come?"

"Yeah, yeah," Gillies exclaims.

Mike gives him directions, then drives out of Downtown and up Bigelow Boulevard, a small highway set on a ridge overlooking the Allegheny River.

The wagon inches along in the rush-hour snarl, but Mike doesn't mind. He glances back and forth between the car ahead of him and the long park that runs along Bigelow. He's spotted a flock of wild turkeys there before. Mike is a city boy with the eye of an outdoorsman. He owns a cabin in the Allegheny National Forest and gets a kick out of seeing wildlife in the city: hawks circling above a cliff beside the Allegheny, deer on the slopes of Mount Washington. One day last year, Mike was visiting his mother's grave on a hillside cemetery that overlooks the Monongahela River when he disturbed a doe grazing nearby. He remembers how the doe dashed away, down the slope and toward the river.

He crosses the Bloomfield Bridge, passing over a quilt of houses that pile down a slope into the ravine below. Bloomfield is a mostly Italian city neighborhood bisected by Liberty Avenue, a busy market street whose shop windows display homemade tortellini and cannoli. Mike turns off Liberty and down a slope to a quiet street, bordered on one side by brick row houses and the other by a ramshackle yellow-brick building with plywood over its windows and a rusted, precarious-looking fire escape.

Waiting for him beside the building are four uniform cops and one city homicide detective. "Mikey Mike!" the detective says.

"Cliffy Cliff!" Mike calls back. "Tell me what you got here."

The detective says three boys were fooling around in the basement of the brick building when they found the bones. The boys are still there, watching the men and looking like they really hope they found something good. They're wearing camouflage fatigues and caps, leather gloves and boots, which reminds Mike of long-ago summer days playing soldier.

Mike puts on gloves and takes a look at the boys' discovery. Two bones, covered in dirt, but definitely porous bone, coupled at a joint. Seven or eight inches long each. One bone is severed smoothly and another has the beginnings of a cut, a saw from the looks of it. They seem too short to be one of the long bones—the arm and leg bones—of a human adult. Could be something else, a child's bone, maybe, Mike's not sure.

Even if they are human, that doesn't necessarily mean there was a homicide. The earth beneath Pittsburgh has been dug and hauled and dumped and flattened and redug so many times over the years that old bones from forgotten burial grounds have surfaced in construction site fill miles away. And since bones can survive for thousands of years, they surface all the time.

When this happens, the first step, after determining that a bone is human, is to reckon its owner's gender, age, height, and time since death—clues that could lead to an eventual identification. An entire skeleton gives a bone expert many clues about gender—the female pelvis, for instance, is generally wider and shallower and the ridges above a male skull's eye cavities thicker. Single bones can be more difficult. One expert who tested his ability to determine the gender of single long bones reported that he was accurate eighty percent of the time. Age at the time of death is easiest to gauge if a skeleton is younger than twenty-five, because not all of the caps at the ends of many bones have fused to the rest of the bones. Different bones fuse at different times, giving death investigators a calendar—for instance, they know that the distal tibia probably will not have begun to fuse unless the subject is between sixteen and nineteen years old. Skeletal changes after the age of twenty-five are more subtle, which makes the age of older skeletons difficult to pinpoint. Height is relatively simple to gauge. Death investigators can estimate height within an inch or two by measuring a single bone—femurs are especially accurate—and applying a formula. Identifying race from skeletal remains requires subtlety, and race is especially difficult to discern in the ethnically mixed United States, but an expert may offer a guess based on skull features. To determine the time since death, investigators will handle bones, sniff them, study them under fluorescent lights, and administer chemical and serological tests. And then there's the low-tech "tongue test"—if your tongue sticks, the bones still contain calcium and are probably less than half a century old.

Investigators use these estimates to cull through missing-persons records. If a potential match is made, then investigators look for a positive identification using X-rays from the missing person's dental or medical records. In 1980, kids playing in a wooded lot in Pittsburgh came across a skull with a bullet hole in it. Forensics experts said the skull probably belonged to a white male, based on the size and shape of the eye sockets. The skull had no jaws, so dental records were no use. The skull sat on a shelf for four years, until a telephone tipster told investigators about a man from the same city neighborhood who had been reported missing in 1979. Fortunately, the missing man had been treated after a motorcycle accident in 1978, and his skull was X-rayed. A comparison between the bullet-pierced skull and the X-rays showed a match. The man's widow confessed to shooting the man while he slept on the couch. Her son cut the head off and put it in a bucket. Investigators hypothesized that the family dog took the head out of the house and left it in the woods, where it was found months later.

Some cases continue to confound investigators. When a skeleton lined with decomposing flesh was found in an abandoned railroad tunnel in Homestead, investigators studied missing-person reports from every police department in the county. Dr. Abdul Shakir found no marks of violence during the autopsy, and toxicological tests revealed no drugs or alcohol in the body's system. The pelvis appeared to be female, and partially fused caps where her ribs met her sternum suggested she was in her early twenties. Strands of fine hair indicated that she was probably white.

The case had its first real break when a forensic odontologist studied the teeth and found a stainless steel crown on the first molar on the left side. Dental crowns in the United States are custom-made out of gold or silver, he told investigators. This crown resembled the generic ones made in Eastern Europe. Detectives questioned a group of Russian and Eastern Europeans living in a public housing project in Homestead, but no strong leads surfaced. Next, the coroner's office shipped the woman's skull to the FBI forensics laboratory in Washington, D.C., where experts measured and cast a replica of the woman's face in clay. Five months after the skeleton was found, Dr. Cyril Wecht held a press conference, waving a drawing of the FBI model in front of television cameras while a Russian teacher from the University of Pittsburgh translated his words. But despite all these efforts, the trail has grown cold and the woman's identity remains unknown.

Mike tells the detective he suspects the bones aren't human. Still, he wouldn't mind checking out this basement. "Let's go in and see what else we find," he says.

"You got suits in the wagon?" a beefy uniform cop asks. "It's dirty as hell down there."

"Cliff, why don't you just go on down there and bring up whatever you find," Mike tells the detective, who is wearing an expensive-looking suit and a red pinstriped dress shirt. Mike's joking, of course. He would never pass on the chance to root around in an abandoned building for old bones.

The detective laughs, then frowns as he sees the beige van pull up and the three men getting out with their equipment. "What the hell is this?" he says. "Who the hell are these people?"

"Oh, that's MSNBC," Mike says. "They're all right. They're gonna go in with us."

The detective relaxes, but everyone puts on their somber camera faces and looks elsewhere as the outsiders approach. No introductions are made. The cops distribute flashlights and tell the boys to show them where they found the bones. The boys scramble up a vine-entangled hillside next to the building. Mike and the cops follow more slowly, grabbing signposts to haul themselves up. Gillies doesn't follow, but the cameraman does. The boys point to a narrow opening where the brick wall has collapsed, and the men duck through, into the darkness. The boys and the middle-aged cameraman stay behind.

The basement smells rich and earthy. The heavy-duty police flashlights show a wooden ceiling and a dirt floor cluttered with planks, pipes, and metal drums. A brick chimney runs from the ground to the ceiling, and a trapdoor in it is leaking a big soft pile of soot. That's where the boys found the bones, one of the cops says, his voice echoing in the darkness.

Taking care not to bump his head, Mike begins nudging his boot through the pile, the detective aiming the flashlight at it for him. He picks up a long bone-shaped object with a jointlike edge. In the darkness, it's hard to make out. Mike scrapes off the dirt for a better look.

"That bone?" the detective mutters. "That ain't bone."

"That's pipe," Mike and the detective say simultaneously. Mike taps it against a large metal pipe, and the distinctive *tink-tink* of metal on metal clinches it.

Mike starts rooting around again, but the earth is too heavy to move with his foot. A cop hands him a shovel and Mike asks him if he found it in the basement.

"The boys had it," the cop says.

"Those boys are well prepared," Mike says.

"I noticed that," the detective says.

"When I first saw them, I thought there was a little mini-militia down here," Mike says.

Mike digs for a few more minutes, unearthing a few more chunks of metal pipe. Finally, he suggests that he take the bones back to the office and let the pathologist on duty tomorrow morning take a look. If they're human, they'll come back and do a thorough dig. "The bones they found look like animal to me, but I'm not an anthropologist," Mike says.

"Hmm," the detective says, mock-impressed. "You looked up that word before you left the office, didn't you? *Anthropologist.*"

Mike laughs. "I'm not the bone collector. You saw that movie, right? About the girl?"

"That was such a bullshit movie," the detective says.

"I didn't see it," Mike says.

"Crime techs would love it," the detective says. "It was all about crime techs."

"So that's what we'll do," Mike says. "If it turns out to be something, we'll come back tomorrow and they can spend the rest of the day sifting through this dirt."

"All righty," the detective says.

"Dig and sift, dig and sift," Mike says.

Mike and the cops shine their flashlights around the cellar, noting an old-fashioned wooden skateboard among the debris. Reflexively, they begin fashioning theories.

"So some kid was skateboarding," Mike says. "He slipped and fell through the chimney and these are his decomposed remains." This reminds Mike of an old case. "Remember that kid from Mount Washington? He fell down a chimney trying to break into a school?"

"Oh yeah!" the cop exclaims. "Yeah, yeah, yeah."

"They found him like five, ten years later when they did some furnace work on the chimney," Mike says. "Well . . . I can't see us digging in here for no good reason. I can't see anything else that looks like evidence."

"We'll let the *anthropologists* figure it out," the detective says.

When they come back out, Gillies is interviewing the three boys, two eleven-year-olds and one sixteen-year-old. They were busy digging a trench when they noticed the opening in the brick wall, the boys said.

"We were flashing our flashlights and all," one boy says, "and we picked up a bone and we took it up to . . . "

A second boy interrupts: "We took it up to my house, and showed it to my sister. She just got out of nursing school, and we asked her if she thought it was a human bone. She said it might be a human bone, but it was kind of small so it was either a kid's bone or a female."

"What did it look like to you?" Gillies asks.

"It looked like an elbow bone," the second boy says.

"What did you think when you saw it?" Gillies asks.

"I didn't know what it was," the first boy says.

"I was like: 'Give me that, man—we should ask somebody if it's human,' " the second boy says.

Meanwhile, Mike has taken another look at the bones and is even more certain they're not human. One has an odd knob on the end that looks unfamiliar to him. Mike talks it over with the detective, and then the detective asks Mike why MSNBC is following him around.

"They're doing a new show," Mike says. "Something like *Cops*, something about death investigators."

"That's you, man," the detective says.

"Right," Mike says. "Death investigator extraordinaire."

Gillies interviews Mike next. Mike gives a concise rundown of the case and his plan to show the bone to a pathologist. The only problem is he keeps looking directly at the camera. The first time he does so, Gillies waves his arms wildly to get Mike to look his way. But Mike keeps looking back into the lens. Each time, Gillies takes two fingers and points at his own eyes in a *look-at-me* gesture.

Not that it matters much. No matter how good the tape is, the case is most likely just another scoop and run. No massive exhumation project. No ancient murder to solve. Today, like most days, death investigation does not make for great TV.

But Mike seems content as he gets into the wagon to head back to the office. A nothing case, but enjoyable anyway. He got to chat with the cops, and he got to mess around in that dark cellar, looking for bones. Not that different from the boys playing soldier.

As Mike turns back onto the Bloomfield Bridge, the wagon's cell phone rings. Mike picks up. "Bones-R-Us?" he says into the receiver, grinning at his own joke.

EIGHT

THE FLOATER

He was a short, pudgy man, forty-six years old and 190 pounds soaking wet. He lived on a houseboat on the Allegheny River near the Pittsburgh Zoo. He'd lived there since about the time he broke up with his girlfriend, several weeks ago. He went into the water sometime within the last few days, less than a week ago, more than a day. He may have been pushed, but his body bore no marks of violence. He drank a lot, so perhaps he fell in or went for a drunken swim. Maybe he jumped, distraught over his girlfriend. At any rate, he died, probably from drowning.

The water was cool, around seventy degrees. Fed by dozens of tributaries, the Allegheny River runs south from southwestern New York to downtown Pittsburgh, where the Monongahela joins it to form the Ohio. If the man fell off his houseboat or jumped off the nearby Highland Park Bridge, his body would have drifted downstream a few hundred yards and tumbled unnoticed over the Number Two Lock and Dam before continuing around the long final bend of the river. This stretch of city river, called the Lower Allegheny, is as wide as three football fields end to end. Round tree-covered hills rise on both sides of the river, and all the flat spots are clustered with houses.

At first, his lungs still held pockets of air, so he probably floated for a while. Then, as time passed and water seeped in through his open mouth and nose, the air pockets bubbled out as foam. Water saturated his lungs and his body sank, his heavy head, legs and arms hanging down, his butt high.

At the bottom of the nine-foot channel dredged for coal barges, the body slow-rolled through the fine sooty sediment left after the dredgers' massive clamshell buckets had dug out all the sand and gravel. The river nudged him downstream.

Finding no resistance from the body's immune system, bacteria in the body began to feed and reproduce. Down on the river bottom, the water was cooler, which slowed the bacterial activity. But decomposition did continue, and gases formed in the dead man's intestinal tract. The gases built up, bloating the man's abdomen and lifting his body from the river bottom and gradually to the surface.

A little after 4:00 p.m., a boater spotted the dead man floating face-down in the river near Washington's Crossing Bridge, almost three and a half miles from his houseboat. A family water-skiing nearby saw the boater idling in the middle of the river and wondered if he was having engine trouble. The water-skiers came over to see if he needed help, and the boater pointed out the body. The father of the water-skiers had a cell phone, and he called 911. The emergency operator radioed the city police's river rescue division, which dispatched a boat and two officers.

In the WTAE-TV Channel Four newsroom in Wilkinsburg, a reporter heard the river rescue call over the police scanner. A floater near Washington's Crossing Bridge. The reporter dialed the Allegheny County Coroner's Office to find out what was going on.

Police reporters on deadline at the local papers and television stations call the coroner's office at the same time every evening to check on the night's mayhem. Ed and Mike are friendly with some of the reporters and feel a particular kinship with the ones who work the evening shift. Other reporters they distrust. Ed doesn't forget when he's been burned. Sometimes reporters find out about a death and call just as the deputy coroners are heading to a scene. If they're television, Ed instructs them to get his good side on camera.

But when the phone rings in the investigative office this afternoon, Mike is shuttling Dr. Cyril Wecht to a speech and Ed is showing the MSNBC gang around the autopsy room, so Tracy McAninch picks up. She says she hasn't heard anything and hangs up the phone. "That was Channel Four," Tracy tells Carey. "They're asking if we know anything about someone in the river."

Fifteen minutes later, the phone rings again. By now, Ed is back. This time, it's a city homicide detective, the same one who caught the bone case in Bloomfield. He tells Ed about the body, which river rescue officers have by now fished out of the water and brought to a small dock. He gives Ed directions to the dock and he and Mike take off, TV people and interns in tow.

The caravan of two coroner's wagons and the beige TV van head up the river, then double back underneath the building-sized concrete abutments of Washington's Crossing Bridge. The sky-blue arch bridge was built in 1923, and its name commemorates the December day in 1753 when a young George Washington narrowly avoided becoming just another Allegheny River floater himself. On a diplomatic mission, Washington fell into the icy water from his raft but managed to scramble to a tiny island on this section of the river, where he spent a frigid night before continuing his journey.

On this summer day almost 250 years later, the riverbank is tree-lined and the air is pleasantly cool. When the caravan pulls up, a row of reporters and cameramen are already waiting. ("Ooh, the locals are here," Trent Gillies, the MSNBC producer, says to the sound technician. "Everybody in town.")

A towboat and a set of barges containing black mountains of coal are muscling upriver as Mike and Ed and the others file down a wooden gangplank to a floating metal dock that runs parallel to the riverbank. Tied to the dock is the river rescue boat, dwarfed by a big red, white, and blue sternwheeler. Two police officers in shorts and orange life jackets stand wide-legged in the river rescue boat, which is equipped with side panels that lower so they can easily yank bodies—living or dead—on board. The homicide detective stands on the dock, next to a blue body bag.

Everyone greets each other as waves from the coal barge's wake begin slapping at the dock, rocking the river rescue boat. Both Mike and Ed know the detective and Mike also knows one of the river rescue cops. As usual,

Ed and Mike do not need to confer about who will do what; they've been working together long enough to know.

Ed starts quizzing the detective. The body was found a hundred yards upriver. The river rescue cops pulled him out of the river and bagged him. The dead man was carrying identification in his waterlogged brown wallet, and the detective has already checked to see if a missing-person report has been filed under the floater's name. None has.

As the cameraman rolls tape and the interns watch, Mike unzips the body bag, which exhales a rich bouquet of river mud and early-stage stinker.

"The wind's going your way," one river rescue cop warns the homicide detective, who nods but doesn't move. He's smelled plenty worse than this.

The floater lies on his stomach. Mike turns him over, revealing a flattened-looking gray face, askew nose, closed eyes and matted hair and mustache. The floater's cut-off jeans shorts and T-shirt are blackened with sooty river sediment, which means he was rolling around on the bottom a while. He's been dead long enough to sink to the bottom and rise back up. He lifts the floater's shirt and studies his torso for signs of trauma—nothing.

As a kayaker cuts through the water on his red spearlike craft, Mike and Ed talk it over and decide to get the body onto a gurney down here on the dock, away from the local news cameras. Mike begins wrestling off the floater's rings—the fingers are purple and thickened from the water—while Ed takes inventory of the dead man's scant possessions, which will be taken back to the office and temporarily stored in the walk-in safe on the second floor of the coroner's office.

"We've got a white ring . . . a yellow watch . . . another white band," Ed says, as Mike removes each item and places them in a plastic baggie. "No necklace. No earrings."

Deputy coroners must be painstaking in this inventory process. They're careful because the stereotypical image of the thieving morgue worker still exists. Relatives keep a sharp eye on deputy coroners when there is cash at the scene, and they will raise hell if they think a body has been looted. In fact, just this past March, a woman told Philadelphia police that someone was using her dead father's credit cards to rent cars and buy computer equipment. Police arrested two suspects, who said they bought the cards from Philadelphia medical examiner's employees who worked the death scene. Using that evidence, police mounted a sting operation against three Philadelphia morgue workers. A police detective planted a bag of money at a death scene and busted the morgue worker who stole it. Two other medical examiner workers were charged with stealing more than $90,000 in cash and property from the dead over the past decade.

So an honest deputy coroner must create a paper trail. That's why Ed got so upset with himself a few days ago, when he got back to the coroner's office and saw that he'd overlooked a ring on the finger of the obese dead woman—he hadn't noted it on the inventory at the scene, as protocol dictates. He called the woman's husband immediately and apologized. About a year before Ed joined the coroner's office, an anonymous tipster called the coroner and said that two coroner's office employees stole money from a man killed on a local highway. The coroner's staffers documented and turned over $3,100, but the tipster said they pocketed more money. State police investigated, but came up with no evidence. One of the accused, a veteran deputy coroner who has since retired, insisted the charges were false.

Deputy coroners cover their backs by using nondescript terms in their inventory lists. As Tiffani explained to an intern a few months ago, "Never, ever, ever use the word 'leather.' It might be leather, but you don't know for sure. Don't say it's a gold watch, say it's a yellow watch. If the family gets the watch and it tarnishes, they could say that you said it was gold and you could be in trouble. If something is silver, say it's white. Even if you *know* it's marijuana, say it's a green, leafy substance."

Despite the perils of dealing with money and valuables, it's one of the interesting aspects of the job. Tiffani worked a case last month in which an elderly woman had 1,160 one-dollar bills hidden around her house. This, of course, led to speculation among the deputy coroners that the septuagenarian was a stripper. "She did all the nursing homes," one suggested. Then there was the homeless man who kept ten different wallets hidden away in his clothing. Deputies went through the wallets, counting more than $6,000. At another death scene, deputy coroners spent hours counting $4,000 in cash—$1,600 of which was in coins.

After digging through the floater's sodden pockets, Mike reports that the body bears no such riches.

"Three dollars in his left front pocket," Mike tells Ed. "No credit cards."

The detective watches the deputy coroners work.

"So what was up with them bones the other day?" he asks Mike.

"They were animal bones," Mike says. "Probably dog bones."

"Somebody tortured Lassie?" the detective suggests.

Gillies interviews the river rescue cops. Ed instructs Tracy on how to take photos of the scene. Mike finds a soggy Veterans Administration card in the wallet, which could be a good source of information. They'll call the VA back at the office and have the floater's hospital records sent over. This could lead to information about the dead man's medical history and also perhaps an emergency-contact phone number that could help them track down a next of kin.

After zipping up the body bag, Ed gets the feet and Mike the head and they load him onto the gurney and wheel it up the steep wooden gangplank. Ed is walking backward, tugging the gurney up the ramp, when he stumbles, right in view of the cameras. Everybody sticks to the no-grinning-near-dead-bodies-on-camera rule, although Ed knows he's going to take some ribbing later for his near-fall.

They shove the gurney into the wagon and a television reporter sidles up to Ed. "So what you got, Ed?" the reporter asks. "Can you tell us anything?"

Ed might have given him a tidbit or a quick quote, except that no family had been found. One of the worst blunders a deputy coroner can make is break the news to a family via the television news. "Not yet," Ed says simply.

"No foul play or anything?" the reporter presses.

"I can't tell you anything about that 'til the autopsy," Ed says. He points the reporter toward the homicide detective.

Back at the investigative office, information trickles in all evening. First Ed calls the police in the township where the man used to live and asks them to go to the address listed on the driver's license. The police find nobody home.

Then Ed calls the VA. The floater was treated a year ago, according to VA records. The wall of his aorta had weakened and the pressure of blood ballooned it into a small sac, which doctors removed and repaired. He also was admitted to a VA detox center for alcohol problems. Furthermore, VA records listed the floater's mother as his next of kin, which gives Ed an address.

He calls state police, who go to the mother's address and tell her to call Ed. The dead man's mother tells Ed that her son moved to the houseboat several weeks ago after breaking up with his girlfriend. Ed calls the girlfriend, who says the dead man never talked about suicide.

Mike teases Ed about his on-camera stumble on the gangplank. Mike says he never backs into the cameras when he's moving a gurney. "Gotta show the good side," Mike says.

"I don't *have* a good side," Ed says mournfully.

Ed also gives an interview about the case to the MSNBC crew. He sits in his usual seat, his round and sunburned face aglow in the TV lights. When Ed is asked to estimate how long the body was in the water, he explains the process of decomposition gas building up in the intestinal tract. The exterior of the body, though gray and waterlogged, looks much more intact than a body lying in the open air for several days, he explains, because the water keeps it cool. However, bacteria are working busily away on the interior. After a night out of the water in the cooler, the decomposition will be markedly more advanced. So Ed said he would guess the body's been in the water more than three days and less than seven. "That's what I think," he says. "What do you think, Mike?"

Mike looks unwilling to be dragged into a debate about such an inexact science, especially on camera, but the decomposition just doesn't look that far advanced to him. "I think maybe a day or two," he says.

"Oh, really?" Ed says.

They don't debate it further. Both know that only the autopsy will provide more clues as to the time of death, not to mention shedding light on whether foul play was involved. As usual, the answers are hiding inside the body.

The next day, the ribbing begins when a senior deputy coroner stops into the investigative office while Ed is tapping out a story on a woman who died in the hospital when she yanked a catheter out of her neck. "Nice footage last night," the senior deputy says. He feigns pushing a gurney and stumbling exaggeratedly. "Caught you tripping."

"I tried to make it an action shot," Ed says.

Ed is working the day shift today. After getting off at eleven o'clock last night, a phone call woke him at home at 5:00 a.m. It was an overnight-shift deputy, saying they needed someone to fill in on the day shift. Someone had called off. Ed said OK, and then lay in bed, knowing he wouldn't be able to fall asleep, since the day shift started at 7:00 a.m. So he got up and came in half an hour early. Ed might as well get used to the day shift since he is switching over permanently next week.

Ed and Mike will miss working and debating cases together, but they have hardly discussed the fact that Ed is switching to the day shift in nine days. Mike didn't even find out about it from Ed. Another deputy had told Mike about the shift change while Mike was off on bereavement leave after his father died. Mike has been expecting such a change for a while, with Ed's kids getting older and all, but he knows he will miss working with Ed. Part of the reason they work so well together, Mike reasons, is that they share similar qualities—easygoing attitudes, the ability to handle any case, medical backgrounds. And then there's the indescribable bond that comes from seven years of working side by side, seeing it all together. Mike knows he won't find another partner like Ed.

When Don and Sis pull the floater out of his waterlogged body bag and onto the autopsy table, bloody foam bubbles from his mouth. Pathologists have tried for many years to identify an incontestable sign of drowning, and this white or red-tinged froth coming from the mouth is the closest they've gotten. The drowner's gasping lungs gulp in water, which mixes with air, producing froth. But it's not a perfect clue. Some drowning victims do not froth, and occasionally other victims do, including some victims of heart disease or drug overdoses. Other drowning signs are unreliable. Sometimes the lungs are waterlogged, other times overinflated. The stomach may contain watery fluid or even silt or weeds, but that doesn't mean the victim died from drowning. Histological and chemical testing have proved inconclusive. If the victim is clutching rocks or weeds from the water bottom, that could be interpreted as a sign of drowning, since he or she presumably went into the water alive.

Some drowning victims absorb a large volume of water, some very little. The lungs seem to be capable of soaking a large amount of water into the circulatory system, where the heart and kidneys manage the overload. In other cases, a small amount of water enters the trachea and the larynx automatically spasms, producing a thick mucous plug that keeps air from entering the lungs.

But by the time a waterlogged corpse is on the autopsy table, signs of drowning have faded away. So Dr. Shaun Ladham knows he likely will not find a cause of death today. He needs to rule out that someone poisoned, beat, or forced the floater into the water. If no such evidence is found, the case will be called a suicide or an accident. But for now, unless some obvious trauma is found that points to homicide, the case will be pending until lab results come back and the pathologists can huddle over the evidence.

As Ed predicted yesterday, decomposition has advanced overnight. The dead man's stomach is green and so distended that his wet T-shirt is riding up. Bacteria from the lungs and intestines have crept up and down the dead man's vascular system, darkening the blood vessels so that a purple tracery webs his arms and legs. His face looks puffy, giving him a piggish look, his eyes squeezed shut. Sis dries his face and smoothes his mustache for the photos. When she cuts away his muddy T-shirt and cut-off jeans shorts, pockets turned inside-out by the deputy coroners the day before, his scrotum is hugely distended and misshapen with gas, swelled to the size and approximate shape of a large apple. The floater is wearing no underwear—a common characteristic of suicide victims, if you believe the deputy coroners, but hardly something that Ladham can cite as evidence for the autopsy report. (Deputy coroners also insist that a larger than expected number of dead people are wearing nothing when they expire.)

Just as Ladham finishes the external examination—which reveals nothing troubling, just old scars from ankle and knee surgery—the door buzzes and in walks Dr. Cyril Wecht, his unknotted tie flapping free as usual.

Ladham greets his boss and says: "This is the guy who lived on a houseboat."

"They found him in the water, right?" Wecht says.

"Yeah, but we don't know how he got there," Ladham says. "So it will probably be a pending."

"Until you find a subdural, right?" Wecht says, grinning.

Ladham grins too at the idea of a case being so dramatic and easy—a suicidal or accidental drowning case suddenly becoming a homicide when you pop the skull and find a subdural hemorrhage and it turns out someone smacked him with a two-by-four. Like something on TV . . . or one of the freak cases in the medical journals or popular pathology books.

And yet, despite their wry faces, Ladham and Wecht both know it can happen that way, and not only on TV. There's always a chance. The moment Wecht leaves the autopsy room, Ladham turns to the floater's head. He tweaks the nose to see if it was broken, thumbs open the red eyes, and massages the wet head with his palms, feeling for skull fractures. Nothing, of course.

When Sis cuts his torso open, the decomposition is obvious. The floater's insides are a mess—the reds of muscle and organs fading into the yellows of fat, everything merging. Sis easily draws a full tube of urine out of his bladder, a sign he may have been drinking just before he drowned. Lab tests will say for sure. Sis removes the heart and lungs and then frees the liver, which is spotted with white nodules. "Shaun, he's got cirrhosis," Sis calls to Ladham, who is now talking it over with Dr. Abdul Shakir.

The pieces are coming together. No sign of trauma yet. A full bladder. A history of drinking. Cirrhosis of the liver. Living on a houseboat upriver from where they fished him out.

"OK, so the guy was a drinker," Ladham tells Shakir. "So he got stoned, and fell in. Or he decided to go in."

Don is showing a new autopsy tech how to cut open a skull. He keeps up a steady stream of advice as she struggles to cut a smooth circle around the head. Then Don tells her to insert the hooked end of a hammer into the cut and yank. "Like you're starting a lawnmower," Don says.

Just as she pops the skull, Ed Strimlan wanders into the autopsy room. He is gratified to see that his prediction about the floater was right—the guy's all green and his brain is mush. Floaters always look worse the next day, especially when they've spent a few days in the water. No way he'd only been in the water one day, like Mike said. He couldn't forget to tell Mike.

The techs lift out the soggy mess of brain, and Ladham takes a break from another body and comes over to take a look. No obvious subdural bleeding or damage to the brain itself, but the brain is in such bad condition it's hard to be sure. He finds hemorrhages in the temporal bones of the skull. Drowning victims often have the small blue patches, although the hemorrhages too aren't considered an indisputable sign of drowning.

Ladham prods the head, leans over to peer into the cavity, the base of the skull, searching for a sign of fracture. Nothing. He grabs the inside walls of the skull with both hands, yanking hard, looking for that tiny hairline crack to open and show itself. Nothing. But Ladham is not quite satisfied. It's too messy in there to see as well as he wants to.

By now, with everything pointing toward a typical drunken drowning, Wecht's half-joking prediction of foul play seems like the longest of long shots. And the body on the other side of the autopsy room is awaiting Ladham's time and attention, not to mention all the unfinished autopsy reports and toxicology screenings and histology slides in his office. But then again, catching the long shots is what the job is all about, catching the cases that elude everyone else, the police, the family members, even good deputies like Mike and Ed. What if everybody missed something? If it weren't for the long shots, this job wouldn't exist.

So Ladham grabs a hose and flushes out the inside of the skull, and peers in again. Then he swabs the inside of the cavity with a paper towel, running it over all the curves and ridges, and looks again. He prods and squints and manipulates, again and again, doing the painstaking job of a good forensic pathologist: searching for a killer that just might exist.

NINE

PICKLES IN COURT

The coroner's office is bustling today, preparing for the inquest into the shooting death of the man in the Hill District. Deputy sheriffs are bringing in Pickles any minute now, and Smitty is getting slammed.

The inquest is scheduled to begin in fifteen minutes, and Deputy Coroner John Smith is the only one in the investigative office. That means Smitty is simultaneously waiting for Pickles's arrival, ordering Dr. Wecht's lunch, teaching Tracy McAninch how to run the elevator for the inquest, finding keys to move Dr. Rozin's car out of the garage so they could bring in the suspect, and looking up information about a case for Dr. Ladham. Then the bat light starts blinking. That's what the deputies call the red light on the wall in the investigative office that blinks when the garage door opens downstairs. Smitty looks at the security camera monitor that shows a blurry black-and-white image of the basement. Three shadowy figures are walking in.

Smitty is startled. He is expecting a sheriff's patrol car bearing Pickles to arrive down there any minute, but they wouldn't just stroll in like this. Smitty bolts downstairs, where he runs into an administrator and a janitor, who are escorting a teenaged boy to the elevator. They tell Smitty that the boy is a witness in the case and they didn't want to bring him in through the front lobby, where a noisy group of Pickles's friends and family are waiting to go up to the courtroom. It's hard enough to get witnesses to testify these days without intimidating them, so they're going to run him up in the elevator.

Tracy is still a bit wobbly on the timing of the lever that stops and starts the elevator, but she's glad to have a job to do.

It's been a week since the guy in Tracy's neighborhood shot himself in the mouth, a week of questions from friends and neighbors. It seemed like everybody was talking about it. Now she's about to watch the culmination of the shooting that happened on her very first night at the coroner's office. Tracy is curious to watch the inquest. Someday, if she works in a crime lab, she'll testify in cases like this. Everybody is running late for the inquest, which is supposed to start at noon. At 11:55 a.m., two deputy sheriffs arrive and begin running handheld metal detectors over people waiting to go up to the courtroom. One by one, the crowd in the lobby thins as people trudge up the wide marble steps to the third floor.

At 12:05 p.m., the sheriff's patrol car pulls into the basement with Pickles. Deputy sheriffs close the garage door, pull the tall man out of the back seat and walk him down a long dark concrete hallway, the one the witness traveled twenty minutes ago, to the elevator. Inside, they make him face the rear of the elevator for the trip to the third floor. Upstairs, they walk him to the bullpen, where he will meet with his attorney. In high-profile cases, news photographers wait in this hallway and position themselves in front of the elevator when they hear it start to creak upward. When the elevator doors rattle open, the TV lights click on and photographers snap pictures of the blinking defendants. But that doesn't happen in this case. No reporters or photographers are here today.

At 12:15 p.m., the assistant district attorney, Thomas Merrick, approaches the victim's mother, the woman who fainted in the crying room two weeks ago. She introduces him to her daughter. "How you doing?" Merrick says, then catches himself. "I'm sorry for your loss," he says quickly. The defense attorney, Lee Rothman, follows suit, introducing himself to the ten people who are here for Pickles, including a woman who says she's his sister. The Pickles group is joking around, as Pickles did during the arraignment.

At 12:20 p.m., the deputy sheriffs escort Pickles into the courtroom. He's wearing a white T-shirt underneath his red jail jumpsuit. One of the women in his group calls out to him: "Hey, baby!" This infuriates one of the coroner's office administrators, who moves threateningly toward the offender and barks: "Let's have some order, please!" A small grin crosses Pickles's face as he sits down at the defense table. Now facing away from his people, he sucks in his lips and puts on a disinterested look.

A moment later, Timothy Uhrich sweeps into the courtroom. Uhrich, a deputy coroner and attorney for the coroner's office, fills out the shoulders of his dark robe, and his fleshy, squarish head suits the magisterial garment, although his voice and eyes are mild. Uhrich will decide today whether the district attorney's evidence is strong enough to send the case to trial at the courthouse a block up Ross Street. If not, Pickles will go free.

Uhrich takes a seat behind the judge's dais. He introduces himself and gives an overview of the case—the names of the defendant and the victim, the time and place of death. "The postmortem examination was performed by Dr. Leon Rozin, who gave the immediate cause of death as gunshot wound of the chest," Uhrich says. "The certification of identification was made by the mother of the deceased."

At Uhrich's matter-of-fact words, the dead man's mother holds a tissue to her eyes and a woman next to her pats her arm and rubs her shoulder.

Two plainclothed detectives and one uniformed police officer stand and lift their right hands to be sworn in as potential witnesses. All of them will not be needed unless things go very badly for Merrick, the prosecutor. In many inquests, the district attorney calls only one witness, particularly if the cops have a solid confession or eyewitness. The prosecution's job is easier in coroner's inquests than in the homicide trial that may follow. In an inquest, the district attorney must show only that it is likely the defendant is the killer, not prove it beyond a reasonable doubt.

But it soon becomes clear that this case is not that easy.

Merrick calls his first witness, Detective Jill Smallwood, to the witness stand. The young, pretty homicide detective takes a seat in the wooden box and adjusts the microphone, which is bound with duct tape. She looks serious and concerned, her eyebrows knit together, as she begins answering questions. Pickles crosses his arms and stares fixedly at Smallwood during her testimony.

Merrick's questions take the detective through the events of the night of June 5. At 9:13 p.m., shots were heard in the housing project in the Hill District. Smallwood arrived at the scene around 9:30 p.m. Police officers led her to the body lying in the courtyard. At first, police thought he'd been shot in the face because his head was lying in a pool of blood, but it turned out the shot was in the chest. Forty feet away, police found another, smaller pool of blood, a .38-caliber bullet casing, and an uneaten candy bar. They figured that was where the dead man was shot.

Someone in the group of Pickles's supporters sniffs disdainfully when Smallwood mentions the candy bar, as if to say: *That all you got? A candy bar?*

And that is all the evidence Smallwood has to offer the prosecution, because Merrick stops his examination there. Rothman, the defense attorney, takes Smallwood back through her testimony, step by step. He will use the coroner's inquest to dig up as much information about the two-week-old homicide as he can, to probe for weak spots in the prosecution's case. None arise now, but then again, the prosecution has presented no evidence linking Pickles with the killing.

Smallwood takes a seat next to Merrick at the prosecution table. When the next witness enters, a murmur of surprise runs through the audience. It's a teenage boy, thin and barely over five feet, the same boy brought through the basement half an hour earlier to avoid these people. Wearing a blue shirt and jeans, the boy walks over to the witness stand, sits down and slides into a slouched position.

Merrick asks the boy his name, and then asks his age.

"Sixteen," the boy says.

Uhrich, who has been leaning his heavy head on one palm, sits up. "He is sixteen?" he asks.

"Yes, your Honor," Merrick says.

"Is there anyone with him here today?"

Merrick says the boy is currently living at an institution called the Bradley Center because of chronic truancy. A counselor from the Bradley Center is here with the boy, Merrick says.

"My concern is that he is under the age of eighteen, and he is being called to testify in a proceeding," Uhrich says. "I just want to make sure there is someone who is either a parent or *in loco parentis* or a guardian."

Rothman, the defense attorney, sees an opening, a chance to end it all right here, without going to trial. Lose this witness and Pickles could walk free. He stands up. "My concern is, does he want to be here?" Rothman says. "Is he being compelled to testify here? And if so, have his parents been advised of his rights?"

Uhrich says the boy has been compelled to testify by subpoena, like all witnesses. That's not his concern. He just wants to make sure the boy has a legal guardian present.

"But I don't know that a counselor of that facility reaches that status under the laws of the state," Rothman says.

Uhrich says he will allow the boy's testimony and let Rothman fight this battle later. This relieves Merrick, who thanks Uhrich and praises his decency for looking after the boy's interests, and it upsets Rothman, who keeps arguing. "If the witness says, 'I don't want to testify,' is he entitled to have an adult representative present?"

The Bradley Center counselor is his adult representative, Uhrich says.

"But I don't know that I am satisfied with him as a legal guardian," Rothman says.

Uhrich raises his hand and says: "*I* am." And it's over.

During the debate, the boy fidgets with the hem of his blue shirt and squints at whomever is speaking, his head swiveling back and forth. When the questions start coming at him again, he stretches out his legs, dangling them over the edge of the witness box.

"We heard that you are currently living somewhere other than your home," Merrick says. "You are living at the Bradley Center, correct?"

The boy nods.

Uhrich interrupts: "You have to say yes or no."

"Yup," the boy says seriously.

"Prior to that, in particular the day of June fifth, where were you living then?" Merrick asks.

"Home," the boy says.

"Where is home? What community?"

"The Hill," the boy says, squinting at Merrick as if to say, *Don't you know that already?*

"Did you witness, did you observe, something that occurred sometime during the day of June fifth?" Merrick asks.

"What?" the boy asks reasonably.

Merrick simplifies: "Did you see something unusual on the day of June fifth?"

"Yes."

"Physically, if I may ask you, where were you when you saw this event?"

The boy closes his eyes, as if re-envisioning the scene. "Personally, I was at my friend's house." His voice is deep, but it cracks every so often.

It was nighttime, the boy continues. He was hanging out at his friend's apartment in the projects. They heard a popping sound, like a firecracker, and they went to the window to look outside. There, in the lights of the court-yard, two men were tussling. Two black men. The boy knew one of the men and he didn't know the other. The man he knew was grabbing at the other man, who was beating him off. Finally, the other man got loose, and the man he knew fell to the ground. The other man walked away, and the boy saw he had a silver handgun.

As the boy tells the story, he grows more animated. He begins nodding, as if encouraging Merrick to get on with it, to get to the important stuff. Merrick paces back and forth behind the prosecution table. Merrick asks: "Could you describe the way in which he walked away?"

"He walked away with the gun in his left hand," the boy says.

"Slow? Fast? How did he walk away?"

"A little slow, a little fast," the boy says.

"During this event, did you get a good look at the man?" Merrick asks.

"Yes."

"Is that man in this courtroom?" The boy nods affirmatively, then catches himself and says: "Yeah."

"Would you please point to him?" Merrick asks.

The boy stretches a finger at Pickles and, for the first time, flicks a quick look at him. Pickles stares right back at the boy, a slight and disdainful curl on his lips.

So it's pretty much over, but Rothman gives it his best shot. He focuses on the legitimacy of the identification, questioning the boy about how dark it was that night. (It was dark.) Did the fight take place under a light? (No, but the men weren't too far away from one of the lights attached to the brick walls of the project building.) How did the police find out what he'd seen? (He was walking away from the scene and a cop followed him and asked him if he knew anything.) How far away were the men from him? (Pretty far, the boy says.) Rothman jumps on this.

"Was it as far away as a football field?" he asks.

"It was a little closer," the boy says.

"Half of a football field?"

"A little closer."

"That would be fifty yards," Rothman says. "So it was closer than fifty yards?"

"Yes."

"Was it more than ten yards?" Rothman says.

"Yes."

"Was it more than twenty yards?" Rothman suggests.

"No," the boy says.

"So it was somewhere between twenty and ten yards," Rothman says.

"Try fifteen," the boy says.

Rothman cannot find a link weak enough to make a difference in the inquest. He tries to convince Uhrich to allow him to explore what description the boy initially gave of the shooter, but Uhrich says that's an issue for trial, not the inquest. Merrick points out that the boy identified Pickles in a photo array the day after the shooting and he also identified him as the shooter in court today.

That's enough for Uhrich. When Rothman is done and the boy steps down, Uhrich delivers his verdict: "It is my finding that the Commonwealth has made a prima facie case of criminal homicide against the accused, Ernest Harris. He shall be remanded to the custody of the warden of the Allegheny County Jail, and this case is held for court."

Pickles looks bored as the deputy sheriffs put the handcuffs back on. A pregnant woman waves at Pickles as they lead him away, and Uhrich warns her to keep silent. The dead man's mother, who has been breathing fast and shallowly throughout the testimony, and silently cried during Rothman's cross-examination, is led away.

Smallwood heads down to the investigative office, all smiles now, in contrast to her dour testimony earlier. She hugs one deputy coroner, pilfers a couple of french fries from Ed Strimlan, but then grows serious when talk turns to the recent spate of murders. There was a sixty-one-year-old man, shot in the chest. The California man in town on drug business, shot in the chest. Today's case, now headed to trial. A thirty-year-old man shot in the chest. The homeless man Tiffani and Ed had carried up the hill, strangled and beaten to death. A fourteen-year-old boy shot and killed after an argument with an older man. A forty-five-year-old man killed in an accident with a woman who was fleeing police in a stolen van. All in a couple weeks—nothing for Washington or Chicago, but a lot for Pittsburgh.

"There's a shooting every day now," Smallwood says. "They'll shoot you anytime, anywhere."

Tracy watched the inquest from the back row, squeezing in at the last minute. She saw the mother sob and dab her eyes as Uhrich summarized the injuries that had killed her son, and she saw the skinny teenage boy take the stand to challenge the older and harder man. Like everything else in this building, it was a different world from the one she knew.

About a quarter of the way through her internship, Tracy thinks she's figured out how to get through the rest of it. She's heard the same idea over and over: the bodies are debris, junk. The photographer's words: *In the beginning you remember every case, but after a while, you don't remember any of them.* The old lady on her bedroom floor, the overdose with the syringe in his back pocket, the cornea donor, the young homicide from the Hill, the stinker lying among the beer cans, the young suicide with the poem on his computer, the floater. The bodies are nothing more than evidence, the deputy coroners have said over and over.

But Tracy has figured out this much: that approach won't work for her. She understands that most of the interns, like Carey Welch, accept their increasing desensitization as inevitable, a good thing, but Tracy doesn't ever want to entirely lose the reverence she feels when standing over a dead body. Not that she doesn't want the experience to change her. It has changed her. She doesn't wince when the scalpel bites into the skin of the chest. Intellectually, she always knew she would die someday, but seeing the bodies somehow makes it seem more definite.

So she accepts those changes, but she doesn't want to grow too hard, too callous, and lose sight of the fact that there is a family grieving somewhere. Sure, it's easier to view bodies as nothing more than evidence. But Tracy wonders if she loses her softness, what else will she lose?

So last week, when friends and neighbors peppered her with questions about the suicide in her neighborhood, part of her was glad for the reminders.

Maybe, Tracy figured, you *shouldn't* forget something like that.

TEN

ED'S LAST NIGHT

This afternoon, Ed comes in twenty minutes early, beating even Mike to work. A day-shift deputy immediately corners him. "Mister Ed," the deputy says. "County homicide is headed out to Oakdale."

"Nice place," Ed says.

"A kid with a seizure disorder," the deputy continues. "His mother said he hit his head on the TV."

Ed jots down the address and stares at the big wall map, rubbing his lips thoughtfully. He figures he'll wait and he and Mike can go out together, but then an administrator tells him to partner with someone else tonight. Mike and Ed are working with interns and inexperienced deputies tonight, and the supervisor doesn't want his two most veteran deputies gone at the same time.

So when Mike comes in, Ed says: "We're gonna go."

"Where you going?" Mike says.

"A twenty-one-year-old," Ed says. "Hit his head on something."

Ed heads out to Oakdale. The kid had had a seizure disorder since he was ten, Ed finds out. A seizure gripped him at 8:45 a.m., and he collapsed, hitting his head on a television set. His mother gave him his medication and put him to bed. An hour and a half ago, his father came home and found him dead. Everything checks out, and Ed calls in to the office to see if Dr. Shaun Ladham will nix bringing the body in and save the family some grief. Ladham says no, he won't issue a death certificate on this one without at least seeing the body.

Maybe he'll just do an external exam, not the full autopsy, but he wants the body. So Ed brings it in.

And that's how it goes on Ed's last night shift. One body after another, little time for reminiscing or swapping old stories. Mike had considered bringing in a cake, something to mark the occasion, celebrate seven years of a good partnership. But he didn't, of course. He and Ed would still see each other during shift changes.

Ed's not the only person on his last day. Dr. Bennet Omalu's year is up. Next month he moves to the University of Pittsburgh Medical Center, where he will begin a two-year fellowship in neuropathology. During his year at the coroner's office, Bennet realized that a specialization in brain-related deaths would give him an edge. Bennet is foreign, black, and accented. He knows he needs an edge, an ace. Neuropathology will be his ace. Down the road, he may even follow Dr. Cyril Wecht's example and get a law degree.

Before taking off, Bennet stops into the investigative office to say goodbye. Mike is the only deputy there.

"Well, Doc, good luck to you," Mike says. "I enjoyed working with you."

"The pleasure was all mine," Bennet says.

The night continues, and the dry-erase board fills with cases. Ladham is doing autopsies tomorrow, which usually means a heavy night for some reason. Or maybe it's because he has that reputation that they notice when Ladham's on the board and they're picking up a lot of bodies.

Mike and another deputy head out to Point State Park, a triangular Downtown park at the crux of the three rivers. A woman's body in the Monongahela. Unidentified, no age, no medical history. The homicide detectives think she lived under the Fort Pitt Bridge, but matters are further confused when two homeless men start scuffling, one yelling at the other for telling the woman to go into the water.

Mike also catches a suicide call, a thirty-one-year-old man who shot himself in the head. Then Ed gets a thirty-nine-year-old man who dropped dead for no apparent reason at all, a guy who looks in perfectly good shape but keels over playing basketball. Those are the scary ones. Those are the ones you try not to think about too much—especially if you've always carried some extra weight like Ed, or if you smoke and love wings from the Dirty O like Tiffani, or your father had his first heart attack when he was just a couple years older than you are now like Mike. If it can happen to a young, active guy like that . . .

But when you're a death investigator, this series of thoughts has run through your head a thousand times until it's grooved a path in your neural passages, so there's no point in starting down it again. Such thoughts are no longer the revelations that they once were. *In the beginning you remember every case. After a while, you don't remember any of them.*

You just can't ponder this stuff all the time. After hundreds, thousands of bodies, when death-scene jokes have become a habit, about the best you can do is to come up with a catch phrase that you use not only on yourself but on all the people who are curious about your job—and there are lots of people like that, everyone thinks you know some secret. So when someone asks how you deal with constant tragedy, the death of a child maybe, you say that you tell yourself that you are not to blame and you do the job the best you can. Or you tell them that you've learned to separate your life at the deadhouse from the rest of your life. When someone asks whether it's changed the way you view life, you tell them that it's made you more spiritual, maybe even more religious. Or maybe you say the constant tragedy has turned you away from God and reaffirmed your commitment to science-based, manmade justice. Or you explain that it's helped you understand that you are part of the world, not the center of the universe. When someone asks how it's changed your life, you say that you don't drink and drive anymore, you barely smoke at all, you appreciate each day a little more, you hug your kids when you get home at night. You never leave your kids by themselves in the car, not even if you're just running into the drugstore for one second. And you make them wear helmets, always helmets.

(You don't get into how the job seems to change some people in a different way, souring them like a brain soaking in a bucket of formalin. You don't mention how those people grow brusquer with the victims' families, how they start to do things like stabbing a corpse with a liver stick. You don't get into that because that's not you.)

Whether you realize it or not, maybe what eventually happens is that, despite the catch phrases, you don't really change at all. Despite what you've seen, maybe there is a part of you that will never truly acknowledge that someday, sooner or later, *your* own personal and priceless body will be lying exposed on that cold table.

It's your job to deal with death so the rest of the living don't have to. You cover it with a maroon blanket and whisk it away to a deadhouse that looks like a chapel among skyscrapers, where its secrets are laid open.

It's your job to hide death from others—but maybe you get really good at hiding it from yourself as well.

At twenty minutes to eleven, the evening-hitch supervisor plunks down a pile of the new shift schedules, and everybody grabs one. Ed's on days, of course, and a couple of the more amiable day-shift deputies are coming on evenings to work with Mike. Tiffani's switching to day-shift too, and she's happy about it. She never liked the evening shift. Too many bodies, too much waiting around all day for the shift to begin. She'd get up in the morning and then start worrying about having to go into work. It seems to her like the only people who were laid-back enough to actually enjoy the three-to-eleven are Mike Chichwak and Ed Strimlan.

A moment later, a diminutive, pink-cheeked woman in blue scrubs appears at the door and the investigative office goes quiet. The woman is wearing surgical booties, a mask dangles around her neck, and her blonde hair is tucked under a net. She's from the Center for Organ Recovery and Donation, and she's here to harvest the bones of two bodies from earlier tonight, including the gunshot suicide Mike picked up earlier. Her partner is already downstairs in the surgical room, sterilizing it. In a tiny voice, almost a whisper, she says she's ready for the first one.

Ed stands up and says he'll get the body and then he'll just take off for the night. At the door, he pauses and looks down at Mike. "Well, OK," he says.

Mike looks up casually. "I guess I'll see you . . . what? Monday?"

"Monday," Ed says.

"Monday," Mike says.

"OK," Ed says.

Mike searches for words, something that will sum up seven good years. "Well . . . it's been nice."

"OK, then," Ed says. "See ya."

Ed gets the suicide body from the cooler and rides down to the garage with the woman in scrubs. She says there's a small snafu. Nobody has declared the man in the body bag dead. Someone has to officially declare him dead in her presence, so that CORE won't be accused of pronouncing someone dead just so they can harvest the bones. It sounds silly with the man lying inert beside them, but it's necessary.

Ed says he'll be glad to pronounce the man dead. He signs the document and wheels the body across the dim, oil-stained garage. The little woman knocks on a door next to the stinker cooler.

The door opens, revealing a large man in scrubs, a mask concealing his face. He says nothing, no greeting, and the bite of antiseptic fills the garage. Behind the shrouded man is a bright room, the purified walls a brilliant, celestial white.

Ed is about to leave when the CORE woman points at his left arm and says: "What's that?"

A red smudge on his forearm. Blood. "It's him," Ed says, nodding at the body bag. Ed must have brushed the bag and got some blood on him, the dead man leaving one more mark on the living.

Ed has no open cuts, so he's not too worried. "I'm gonna wash this off, if you don't mind," he tells the CORE woman. He squeezes past her to a steel sink nearby. He turns on the water and scrubs the dead man's stain off his arm.

The techs pull the gurney into the sterile room. Ed tells them to take care, and the CORE man, still silent behind his mask, closes the door of the bright room, leaving Ed in the dark garage. Then Ed walks out into the night to get his car and head back to his family, back to his home.

EPILOGUE

Three years after Ed Strimlan and Mike Chichwak parted ways, they have found themselves working side by side once again. After working the day shift for a few months, Ed was promoted to a senior deputy coroner position and moved into the administrative offices on the second floor. Mike was promoted to an equivalent position in 2003. They miss regularly poking around at death scenes, so whenever the office is shorthanded they go out on calls. Their other old evening-shift partner, Tiffani Hunt, now works in the autopsy room as a technician, a more predictable job that better suits her personality. Dr. Bennet Omalu, the former resident pathologist, has returned to the coroner's office as a full-fledged forensic pathologist, with a specialty in neuropathology, his ace in the hole.

The parade of cases has continued, of course, and the coroner's office staffers have long forgotten the ones they worked on in the summer of 2000. Ernest "Pickles" Harris's trial is long over as well; sixteen months after his arrest, he testified that it was a case of self-defense, and a jury acquitted him.

The regular day hours have given Ed the opportunity to pursue his long-term goal of teaching. He now teaches forensic investigation courses at three different colleges: the University of Pittsburgh, Carlow College, and Point Park University. He teaches four evening classes a week, making him just as busy as he was when he was juggling the night shift at the coroner's office with his day job at Trax Farm.

Ed didn't seek out the teaching jobs; the colleges came to him. Asked why there is so much academic interest in forensics programs, Ed says the answer is obvious.

"*CSI*," he says.

By *CSI* Ed means not just the one show, but the horde that followed its success, including the spin-off *CSI: Miami* and an NBC drama called *Crossing Jordan*, about a medical examiner in Boston. Cable television has joined the forensic pathology craze—A&E's *Silent Witness* is a British series about a female pathologist. Documentaries are everywhere, too. HBO has *Autopsy*, Court TV has *Forensic Files*, and TLC has *Medical Detectives*.

The "*CSI* effect," as it's called in the forensics community, is widespread. Now that forensic mysteries can be seen on TV just about every night of the week, thousands of college students are deciding that hunting criminals with science is what they want to do. And colleges and universities are doing their best to accommodate them. The *Chronicle of Higher Education* reports that the boom in interest has led to "higher enrollments, new degree programs, and even a few new faculty jobs." West Virginia University, Oklahoma State University and Carlow College are among those who have developed new degree programs in recent years. Existing programs have exploded; George Washington University's graduate forensics program has doubled in recent years to more than two hundred.

CSI has sparked interest in the field, but it has not created more jobs in crime labs and medicolegal facilities. It remains to be seen whether the growing wave of forensic program graduates will be able to find jobs. Another potential problem with the trend is that the reality of forensic investigation may not live up to expectations created by TV. Much of the time, processing a crime scene is plodding work.

"We have people calling in and emailing us regularly, saying, 'I want to get into criminalistics, where do I go to school for that?' " Ed says. "They think they'll walk out and become an investigator. I try to show them the diversity of the field: ballistics, chemistry, toxicology, pathology. They see guys on TV doing it all."

Ed also has fielded numerous calls at the coroner's office from a novelist who is crafting a thriller featuring a serial killer who is an autopsy technician. Ed enjoys the fanfare his field is getting right now. Others find television's dramatic depictions of forensics downright irritating.

"One thing I don't understand about those programs is why don't they turn the lights on," one deputy coroner says. "Ever notice that? They're always working the scenes with flashlights. Turn a fucking light switch on—maybe that'll help."

Even the autopsy rooms on TV are dramatically dark, whereas the most modern facilities have skylights and big windows: the more natural light that can be shed on the bodies, the better. Another problem is that forensic investigators on television are generalists, specialists in everything from autopsy to fingerprinting. They even interrogate suspects.

Some criminalists fear that the shows will create unrealistic expectations. Victims' families won't understand why crime lab results take two months to come back. Prosecutors won't be willing to go to trial unless they have infallible scientific proof. Juries won't understand that scientific evidence is not always black or white.

Cyril Wecht, for one, rarely watches the shows himself.

"I find them totally absurd, especially the celerity with which things are accomplished," Wecht says. "But that's OK. I'm not a purist, and I recognize fiction as fiction. Whatever it does to proselytize our field, to publicize it, great."

As one of the field's major proselytizers himself, Wecht at seventy-three is as busy as he's ever been. On a bright October day in 2003, Wecht was on the move as usual. An intriguing new case had come up: an unidentified dead woman found floating this morning in the Allegheny River, wrapped in a blanket and bound with duct tape. A major symposium he'd helped organize—a debate about the JFK assassination—was coming up in November, the fortieth anniversary of the case that launched Wecht's career. His fourth popular forensics book, *Mortal Evidence*, had come out two weeks earlier. He'd spoken on Court TV the night before about the Kobe Bryant rape case; he was scheduled to appear again tonight regarding the homicide of Laci Peterson. And as always, he was consulting on outside cases; in a few weeks he is scheduled to face off against his old friend, Dr. Michael Baden, in a police shooting case in Bethlehem, Pennsylvania. Baden, the former medical examiner of New York City, is testifying for the police; Wecht for the family of the man shot eleven times.

In his office, filled with textbooks, a gray microscope, and black leather sofa and chairs, Wecht spoke about what keeps him going.

"It's one thing to work hard, but it's another thing to be bouncing all these balls: coroner, consultant, teacher, writer, testify here, testify there," Wecht said. "Sometimes it gets a little overwhelming. But I enjoy it very much. I can't think of anything more interesting or exciting. I truly can't. There simply is no other field like this one—my God, think, not only law and medicine and science, but the mysteries and the complex, controversial, contentious, challenging areas and aspects of those fields. You can be a lawyer and write a will or do property, big deal. Or be a doctor and see people and listen to their chests or look up their assholes every day. I'm just saying, somebody has to do that, I don't mean to be a smart aleck. But I'm saying, you know, you've got to do your job right, but no way in the world can it be as challenging as this field."

After consulting with his staff about the floater bound in duct tape, Wecht trotted down the stairs at his usual pace (too rushed, as always, for the elevator), snapping instructions at his staff. He went outside and crossed Ross Street, where he joined an erstwhile political enemy, Allegheny County Executive Jim Roddey, who beat Wecht for the post in 1999. But the men were gathered as allies on this day, and they gripped each other's hands and cracked jokes. They were holding a press conference to announce a new eight-story county government building to be built on the spot where they stood.

Roddey took the microphone first, praising Wecht as "the best coroner of any county in America." Then, with a grin, he said, "I'll be happy in my next term to appoint him as our medical examiner."

Wecht chuckled at this. Taking the microphone, he outlined plans for the new building, the top two floors of which would be devoted to a cutting-edge crime lab. The new space will help the county meet the accreditation standards of the American Society of Crime Laboratory Directors, a certification that will be more and more important in future court cases. In addition, the old morgue will undergo a massive expansion project over the next three years, though its landmark granite exterior will remain untouched. New floors will be built into the old, high-ceilinged chapel area, which now sits empty.

"Most of you who grew up in Pittsburgh as I did will recall the chapel, the second and third floors of that chapel space where we used to go as kids to see the dead bodies," Wecht said.

When Roddey retook the microphone, he said, "I just would remind Cyril that not all of us as kids used to run around looking at dead bodies."

Wecht threw his head back and laughed, and Roddey added: "He always was a little different."

SOURCES

In addition to direct observation and interviews, the book draws from the following sources. Autopsy documents, case reports, and inquest transcripts yielded many details. Brochures, statistical analyses, and newsletters produced by the coroner's office also proved to be useful, particularly the Allegheny County Coroner's Statistical Report 2000. I also consulted Allegheny County's 2000 budget.

In addition to the specific materials cited below, I reviewed hundreds of articles from Pittsburgh's primary newspapers—the now defunct *Pittsburgh Press*, the *Pittsburgh Post-Gazette*, and the *Pittsburgh Tribune-Review*—for details about cases and issues at the coroner's office. I also used these articles to deepen my understanding of the history of the office and its role in the community. Furthermore, I read articles from the following newspapers, news services and magazines: the *ABA Journal*, the Associated Press, the *Columbus* (Ohio) *Dispatch*, *Esquire*, the *Los Angeles Times*, the *Morning Call* (Allentown, Pa.), the *New York Times*, *Omni*, Pittsburgh *City Paper*, *Science*, the (Albany, N.Y.) *Times Union*, and *USA Today*.

Published sources of information are grouped by subject below.

THE HISTORY AND BACKGROUND OF FORENSIC PATHOLOGY AND CORONER'S OFFICES

Alexander, C. Bruce. "Trends in Pathology Graduate Medical Education." *Human Pathology*. 32(7):671, 2001.

Bendann, E. *Death Customs: An Analytical Study of Burial Rites*. Dawsons of Pall Mall, London, 1969.

Clark, David, editor. *The Sociology of Death: Theory, Culture, Practice*. Blackwell Publishers, Oxford, U.K., 1993.

Clarkson, Wensley. *Doctors of Death*. Barricade Books, Fort Lee, N.J., 1992.

Forbes, Thomas Rogers. *Surgeons at the Bailey: English Forensic Medicine to 1878*. Yale Univ. Press, New Haven, 1985.

Gittings, Clare. *Death, Burial and the Individual in Early Modern England*. Croom Helm, London, 1984.

Gonzales, Thomas A., Vance, Morgan, Helpern, Milton, and Umberger, Charles J. *Legal Medicine: Pathology and Toxicology*, 2d ed. Appleton-Century-Crofts, Inc., New York, 1954.

Hanzlick, Randy and Combs, Debra. "Medical Examiner and Coroner Systems: History and Trends." *Journal of the American Medical Association*. 279(11):870, 1998.

Hill, Rolla B., and Anderson, Robert E. *The Autopsy—Medical Practice and Public Policy*. Butterworths, Boston, 1988.

Hunnisett, R. F. *The Medieval Coroner*. Cambridge University Press, Cambridge, U.K., 1961.

Johnson, Julie Ann. *Speaking for the Dead: Forensic Scientists and American Justice in the Twentieth Century* (dissertation). University of Michigan, Ann Arbor, Michigan, 1992.

Marten, M. Edward. *The Doctor Looks at Murder*. Doubleday, Doran and Co., Inc., Garden City, N.Y., 1937.

Mohr, James C. *Doctors and the Law: Medical Jurisprudence in Nineteenth-Century America*. Oxford University Press, New York, 1993.

Noguchi, Thomas T., and DiMona, Joseph. *Coroner*. Simon & Schuster, New York, 1983.

Rhine, Stanley. *Bone Voyage: A Journey in Forensic Anthropology*. University of New Mexico Press, Albuquerque, N.M., 1998.

Smith, Roger D., and Prichard, Robert W. "A Survey of First-year Pathology Residents: Factors in Career Choice." *Human Pathology*. 18(11):1089, 1987.

Sung, Tz'u. *The Washing Away of Wrongs: Forensic Medicine in Thirteenth-Century China* (translated by McKnight, Brian E.). Center for Chinese Studies, University of Michigan, Ann Arbor, Michigan, 1981.

Vance, Richard P., Hartmann, William H., and Prichard, Robert W. "Pathology Trainee Manpower: Historical Perspectives." *Archives of Pathology and Laboratory Medicine*. 116:574, 1992.

DEATH INVESTIGATION

Baden, Michael, and Roach, Marion. *Dead Reckoning: The New Science of Catching Killers*. Simon & Schuster, New York, 2001.

Beard, Jonathan. "The Sniffing Detective." *New Scientist*. 166: 21, 2000.

Di Maio, Dominick J., and Di Maio, Vincent J. M. *Forensic Pathology*. CRC Press, Boca Raton, 1993.

Di Maio, Vincent J. M. *Gunshot Wounds: Practical Aspects of Firearms, Ballistics, and Forensic Techniques*. CRC Press, Boca Raton, 1999.

Geravaglia, Jan C., and Talkington, Billy. "Weapon Location Following Suicidal Gunshot Wounds." *American Journal of Forensic Medicine and Pathology*. 20(1):1, 1999.

Hendricks, James E., and Byers, Bryan. *Crisis Intervention in Criminal Justice/Social Service*, 2d ed. Charles C. Thomas Publisher, Springfield, Illinois, 1996.

Knight, Bernard. *Coroner's Autopsy: A Guide to Non-Criminal Autopsies for the General Pathologist*. Churchill Livingstone, Edinburgh, 1983.

Knight, Bernard. *Forensic Pathology*, 2d ed. Oxford University Press, Arnold, 1996.

Kury, George; Weiner, James; and Duval, Jennie V. "Multiple Self-Inflicted Gunshot Wounds to the Head." *American Journal of Forensic Medicine and Pathology*. 21(1):32, 2000.

Mason, J. K. *Forensic Medicine: An Illustrated Reference*. Chapman & Hall Medical, London, 1993.

Newman, Julliana, and McLemore, Jerri. "Forensic Medicine: Matters of Life and Death." *Radiologic Technology*. 71(2):169, 1999.

Pedersen, Daniel. "Down on the Body Farm." *Newsweek*, Oct. 23, 2000 (p. 50).

Prahlow, Joseph A., Long, Scarlett, and Barnard, Jeffrey J. "A Suicide Disguised as a Homicide: Return to Thor Bridge." *American Journal of Forensic Medicine and Pathology*. 19(2):186, 1998.

U.S. Department of Justice Drug Enforcement Administration. "Heroin." http://www.usdoj.gov/dea/concern/heroin.htm (as of 12/11/01).

Wetli, Charles V., Mettleman, Roger E., and Rao, Valerie J. *Practical Forensic Pathology*. Igaku-Shoin Medical Publishers, Inc., New York, 1988.

THE PSYCHOLOGY OF DEATH INVESTIGATION

Charlton, R., Dovey, S. M., Jones, D. G., and Blunt, A. "Effects of Cadaver Dissection on the Attitudes of Medical Students." *Medical Education*. 28:290, 1994.

de L. Horne, David J., Tiller, John W. G., Eizenberg, Norman, and Biddle, Nola. "Reactions of First-Year Medical Students to their Initial Encounter with a Cadaver in the Dissecting Room." *Academic Medicine*. 65(10):645, October 1990.

Hasch, Mike. "Grim Duty: Deputy Coroners do Essential Job in Darkest Moments." *Pittsburgh Press*, October 20, 1984.

Sanner, Margareta A. "Encountering the Dead Body: Experiences of Medical Students in their Anatomy and Pathology Training." *Omega*. 35(2):173, 1997.

Sewell, James D. "The Stress of Homicide Investigations." *Death Studies*. 18:565, 1994.

Stuhlmiller, Cynthia M. "Occupational Meanings and Coping Practices of Rescue Workers in an Earthquake Disaster." *Western Journal of Nursing Research*. 16(3):268, 1994.

Thompson, William E. "Note on Thorson and Powell: Undertakers' Sense of Humor." *Psychological Reports.* 89:607, 2001.

Thorson, James A., and Powell, F. C. "Undertakers' Death Anxiety." *Psychological Reports.* 78:1228, 1996.

Thorson, James A., and Powell, F. C. "Undertakers' Sense of Humor." *Psychological Reports.* 89:175, 2001.

PITTSBURGH'S HISTORY, NEIGHBORHOODS, AND AFRICAN-AMERICAN COMMUNITY

The extensive newspaper clip files in the Pennsylvania Room at the Carnegie Library of Pittsburgh in Oakland yielded dozens of newspaper stories and other materials that helped me gain an understanding of these subjects. In addition, the following resources were particularly useful:

Sebak, Rick. *Downtown Pittsburgh* (video recording). WQED/Pittsburgh, Pittsburgh, 1992.

Stack, Barbara White. "The Color of Justice." *Pittsburgh Post-Gazette*, May 5, 1996.

Toker, Franklin. *Pittsburgh: An Urban Portrait.* University of Pittsburgh Press, Pittsburgh, 1994.

Trotter, Joe William Jr., and Smith, Eric Ledell, editors. *African-Americans in Pennsylvania: Shifting Historical Perspectives.* The Pennsylvania Historical and Museum Commission and the Pennsylvania State University Press, University Park, 1997.

Black and White Economic Conditions in the City of Pittsburgh: A Benchmarks Special Report. University of Pittsburgh, University Center for Social and Urban Research, Pittsburgh, 1995.

FORENSICS IN POPULAR CULTURE

To research this subject, I studied many newspaper and magazine articles about the *CSI* phenomenon, including those from *Time, Newsweek*, The *Washington Post, San Antonio* (Tex.) *Express-News*, and *Buffalo* (N.Y.) *News*. In addition, I drew from the following books and articles in more depth:

Browne, Douglas G., and Tullett, E. V. *Bernard Spilsbury: His Life and Cases.* White Lion Publishers, London, 1976.

Guinn, Jeff. "Dissecting Patricia Cornwell." *Fort Worth* (Tex.) *Star-Telegram*, November 1, 2000.

Helpern, Milton. *Autopsy.* St. Martin's Press, New York, 1977.

Rosenberg, Howard. "Forensic Series Prove There's Life after Death." *Los Angeles Times*, April 9, 2001.

Simpson, Keith. *Forty Years of Murder.* George G. Harrap and Co. Ltd., London, 1979.

Smallwood, Scott. "As Seen on TV." *Chronicle of Higher Education* 48(45):8, July 19, 2002.

Wecht, Cyril, Curriden, Mark, and Wecht, Benjamin. *Cause of Death.* Dutton, New York, 1993.

Wecht, Cyril, Curriden, Mark, and Wecht, Benjamin. *Grave Secrets.* Dutton, New York, 1996.

TRAINING OF DEATH INVESTIGATORS

Baden, Michael, and Hennessee, Judith Adler. *Unnatural Death.* Random House, New York, 1987.

Clark, Steven C., and National Medicolegal Review Panel. *National Guidelines for Death Investigation.* U.S. Department of Justice, Office of Justice Programs, National Institute of Justice, Washington, D.C., 1997.

Haglund, William D., and Ernst, Mary Fran. "The Lay Death Investigator: In Search of a Common Ground." *American Journal of Forensic Medicine and Pathology.* 18(1):21, 1997.

Hanzlick, Randy. "Coroner Training Needs: A Numeric and Geographic Analysis." *Journal of the American Medical Association.* 276(21):1775, 1996.

Hanzlick, Randy, and deJong, Joyce L. "Level of Agreement between Opinions of Medical Examiner Investigators and Forensic Pathologist Medical Examiners Regarding the Manner of Death." *American Journal of Forensic Medicine and Pathology.* 21(1):11, 2000.

CYRIL WECHT

In addition to information gathered from personal interviews and observation, I learned about Wecht from his own popular forensics books (*Grave Secrets* and *Cause of Death*, cited above) and from *Pittsburgh Press* and *Pittsburgh Post-Gazette* articles dating back to the mid-1960s. Two particularly useful articles were:

Batz, Bob, Jr. "Ask Dr. Cyril, and You'll Get an Answer of Wechtian Proportions." *Pittsburgh Post-Gazette*, October 25, 1999.

Bull, John M. R. "Wecht's Opponent Concedes Defeat." *Pittsburgh Post-Gazette,* October 24, 1995.